"ONE UNITED PEOPLE"

"ONE UNITED PEOPLE"

Essays from the People Sector on Singapore's Journey of Racial Harmony

EDITED BY
KOH BUCK SONG

© 2022 Marshall Cavendish International (Asia) Pte Ltd
Text copyright individual contributors

Published in 2022 by Marshall Cavendish Editions
An imprint of Marshall Cavendish International

All rights reserved

No part of this publication may be reproduced, stored in a retrieval system or transmitted, in any form or by any means, electronic, mechanical, photocopying, recording or otherwise, without the prior permission of the copyright owner. Requests for permission should be addressed to the Publisher, Marshall Cavendish International (Asia) Private Limited, 1 New Industrial Road, Singapore 536196. Tel: (65) 6213 9300 E-mail: genref@sg.marshallcavendish.com
Website: www.marshallcavendish.com/genref

The publisher makes no representation or warranties with respect to the contents of this book, and specifically disclaims any implied warranties or merchantability or fitness for any particular purpose, and shall in no event be liable for any loss of profit or any other commercial damage, including but not limited to special, incidental, consequential, or other damages.

Other Marshall Cavendish Offices:
Marshall Cavendish Corporation, 800 Westchester Ave, Suite N-641, Rye Brook, NY 10573, USA • Marshall Cavendish International (Thailand) Co Ltd, 253 Asoke, 16th Floor, Sukhumvit 21 Road, Klongtoey Nua, Wattana, Bangkok 10110, Thailand • Marshall Cavendish (Malaysia) Sdn Bhd, Times Subang, Lot 46, Subang Hi-Tech Industrial Park, Batu Tiga, 40000 Shah Alam, Selangor Darul Ehsan, Malaysia

Marshall Cavendish is a registered trademark of Times Publishing Limited

NATIONAL LIBRARY BOARD, SINGAPORE CATALOGUING IN PUBLICATION DATA

Name(s): Koh, Buck Song, editor.
Title: One united people : essays from the people sector on Singapore's journey of racial harmony / edited by Koh Buck Song.
Description: Singapore : Marshall Cavendish Editions, 2022.
Identifier(s): ISBN 978-981-5009-62-0 (paperback)
Subject(s): LCSH: Singapore--Race relations. | Singapore--Ethnic relations. | Multiculturalism--Singapore.
Classification: DDC 305.80095957--dc23

Printed in Singapore

We, the citizens of Singapore,
pledge ourselves as one united people,
regardless of race, language or religion,
to build a democratic society
based on justice and equality
so as to achieve happiness, prosperity
and progress for our nation.

Singapore's National Pledge,
recited in schools, and elsewhere,
since August 1966

Contents

11   *Prologue*
       Just "Majority Blind Spots", or Something More?
       KOH BUCK SONG

27   If We Start with Conversations, We Can Go Far
       SALEEMAH ISMAIL

34   What We Must Do, to Begin to Talk About Racism
       NAZRY BAHRAWI

41   Can Singapore's Multiculturalism Return to Its Best Days?
       MATILDA GABRIELPILLAI

51   A Reset Needed for Racial Harmony
       BRAEMA MATHIAPARANAM

66   Can Harmony Inhibit Cohesion?
       VISWA SADASIVAN

75 Look Beyond Colour
KANNAN CHANDRAN

85 Racial Integration: Lessons from a Lifetime
KIRPAL SINGH

91 CMIO: An Anglo-Chinese Perspective
MARGARET THOMAS

98 "One United People":
A View from the Singapore Eurasian Community
ALEXIUS A. PEREIRA

112 "Is He Chinese?"
KENNETH PAUL TAN

121 The Question of "Chinese Privilege"
TAN CHEE LAY

129 Deep Roots, Verdant Leaves:
Inspirations from Sinophone Singapore
TAN DAN FENG

138 "Same Same, but Different":
The Peranakan Experience of a Multiracial Singapore
LINDA CHEE

- 147 Towards a More Conscious and Inclusive Capitalism
  JOYCE LIM

- 156 The Sooner, the Better:
  Fighting a Different Virus of Racial Tensions
  BILLY STEVEN TAY

- 164 Dialogue, Differences and Empathy:
  How Theatre Can Facilitate Deeper Engagement
  with Multiculturalism
  AUDREY WONG

- 178 Beneath Society's Hidden Faultlines
  POH YONG HAN

- 188 Unpacking, and Sharing, Ethnic Privilege
  DANA LAM

- 197 Ageing Well Together:
  Quiet Social Transformation, with Help from
  Racial Harmony
  KUA EE HEOK

- 207 Notes Towards a Few Breakthroughs to True Unity
  LAURENCE LIEN

217 One United Patois: Singlish and Race in Singapore
COLIN GOH

227 *Epilogue*
The "Geometry of Community"
KOH BUCK SONG

PROLOGUE

Just "Majority Blind Spots", or Something More?

KOH BUCK SONG

This collection of essays, *"One United People"*, reflects on Singapore's project to integrate its component communities into one society and nation, and offers a snapshot assessment of the progress on this, since independence in 1965.

Insights are drawn, necessarily, from racially diverse perspectives – Malay, Indian (in its sub-groups: Malayali, Tamil and others), Sikh, "Anglo-Chinese", "Old" and "New" Eurasian, Peranakan, Chinese (Chinese-educated and English-educated) and other ethnicities – making up an ethnic microcosm of Singapore.

Among the book's 21 contributors, the age spread is also well-represented, from seniors of the Pioneer generation to a full-time national serviceman. The gender balance is almost there. There are both "born-and-bred" and naturalised Singaporeans. In the essays, lessons from the past are examined, and evolving challenges of the present analysed. A future is tentatively glimpsed, one that might be closer to "one united people", regardless of race.

But first, a note on punctuation. The title of this book – "One United People" – is, at one level, simply a citation of three words from Singapore's National Pledge, hence the quotation marks.

On a deeper level, the set of inverted commas can serve as a wakeup call – a reminder that racial harmony is not a destination, or end-point, that is ever reachable. Instead, harmony among distinctive ethnicities is a never-ending journey, a task without conclusion. It is an aspiration, an ideal, that every citizen and resident can contribute to, and work towards, every day.

Indeed, how precarious any perceived racial harmony actually is, was put most starkly by Finance Minister Lawrence Wong, when he said that "this harmonious state of affairs will always be on a knife-edge", in a speech at a Conference on New Tribalism and Identity Politics in November 2021, organised by the Institute of Policy Studies and the Rajaratnam School of International Studies.

On topics such as this, the choice of words is always crucial. An earlier draft of the Pledge – suggested by then-Minister for Culture (later Deputy Prime Minister) S. Rajaratnam, in a letter dated 18 February 1966 to then-Minister for Education Ong Pang Boon – reads:

> We, as citizens of Singapore,
> pledge ourselves to forget differences
> of race, language or religion
> and become one united people…

Rajaratnam's version of this oath was framed more provisionally – which is intriguing, and unsurprising, given his noted cultural

Just "Majority Blind Spots", or Something More?

sensitivity. His initial hope, it seems, was, first, for a deliberate act of forgetting – that Singaporeans would push into the backs of their minds what their eyes could see clearly: differences of race, and other differentiating characteristics of humans. Perhaps it is only upon such selective amnesia that any modicum of cohesion can be forged, and held together, in any group of any heterogeneity. Such amnesia is to be exercised consciously, so as to override what might lurk in the sub-conscious.

Also, Rajaratnam's use of the words "and become…" envisages efforts as yet incomplete, ongoing actions as opposed to the imagined fait accompli – almost a done deal, as it were – that is implied in the Pledge's final phrasing, "… pledge ourselves as one united people…".

As a political and arts features journalist at *The Straits Times* in the 1990s, I met Mr Rajaratnam a couple of times. In one conversation, something he said, and reiterated, stuck in my mind. He was adamant that people should recognise, and remember, that, beneath our differently coloured skins, the same type of blood flows through all our arteries and veins.

Harmony among distinctive ethnicities is a never-ending journey, a task without conclusion. It is an aspiration, an ideal, that every citizen and resident can contribute to, and work towards, every day.

So, if racial harmony is not a definite destination but a daily duty, then what follows from this is that the notion of a "post-racial Singapore" – a Singapore free from racial preference, discrimination and prejudice – must surely be an illusion. Being "race-blind" is not something people can easily acquire. There is no "Lasik operation" to clear up the cloudiness of racial prejudice, typically learned from infancy, and further conditioned and reinforced by society.

Just as illusory might be the notion of a "melting pot" – that dream that ethnic differences can be boiled down in the "cauldron" of society, to produce a new "stew", beautifully free of conflict. In Singapore, the approach of assimilation ("melting") has been downgraded in favour of integration (sometimes imagined as a bit like a "mosaic"). To continue the quest for an alternative, more accurate, culinary metaphor, some social scientists have suggested that the old notion of a "melting pot" could be replaced by a "salad bowl", in which the ingredients mix but do not disintegrate – that is, each group retains its own character and flavour, its own consistency and texture.

On top of this, an additional element, especially important to state actors, would be a "salad dressing" that lifts the whole blend – in Singapore's case, the "*rojak* sauce" of national identity.

Metaphors matter because they frame mindsets, and unless mindsets are set right, no mindset shift would be possible, and any progress would be hindered. To help clarify this mindset, the key questions considered in this book are: What might threaten social cohesion? What is needed to keep the peace and enhance harmony? What do people need to understand better? And how can they think, perceive and behave differently?

Singapore's tireless closed-door efforts to sustain harmony

To ensure equilibrium in such a delicate balance, effort is always essential. Before independence, Singapore was like any other nation, susceptible to the lava of chaos that can erupt, at any time, from the craters of ethnic difference. The months of July to September 1964 saw the island's worst-ever race riots in living memory, mostly between the Malay and Chinese communities, resulting in 36 fatalities and injuring another 560 people. But since 1965, amongst the world's league of nations, Singapore has done relatively well on the crucial aspect of holding a society's ethnic components together.

Indeed, multiculturalism is, arguably, the X factor of independent Singapore's admired country brand. There is empirical evidence to place Singapore on top of the world: A 2014 analysis by the Pew Research Center in the US found Singapore to be "the world's most religiously diverse nation". In a more recent study in October 2021 – based on phone interviews with 16,254 adults from March to May 2021, in 16 advanced economies – the Pew Research Center found that fewer Singaporeans (25%) reported conflicts between people of different ethnic backgrounds than nearly any other public surveyed.

This strand of multiculturalism is set to become even richer in diversity in future, given Singapore's steady inflow of immigration and the rising rate of intermarriage between Singaporeans and foreign spouses.

This balance in the "ecosystem of ethnic biodiversity" does not happen by accident, as political office-holders remind the public from time to time. The most interventionist state action is the Housing & Development Board's (HDB) Ethnic Integration Policy, which Senior Minister Tharman Shanmugaratnam called "the most intrusive social policy in Singapore", in an interview with the BBC in 2015.

This policy — typically conceived and executed with more than a touch of Singaporean *kiasuism* ("fear of losing out" in Singlish) — was introduced in 1989 to ensure a more balanced mix of ethnic groups in HDB estates, where more than 80% of the population lives. Limits are imposed on the total percentage of a block or neighbourhood that may be occupied by a certain ethnicity, roughly aligned with the racial composition in the country as a whole.

The aim is to prevent the formation of racial enclaves, which were already emerging in 1989, when then-National Development Minister S. Dhanabalan showed in Parliament an annotated map indicating, for example, Malays gathering in Eunos, Indians around Serangoon Road, and Chinese in Hougang. The policy's stated main objective is to promote racial integration by allowing residents of different ethnicities to live together and interact on a regular basis in public housing.

Complementing this structural mechanism are whole networks of human interventions — Singapore's exterior calm in racial harmony is actually the outcome of much constant effort behind the scenes. At grassroots level, Inter-Racial Confidence Circles were set up in 2002 — in the wake of the 9/11 attacks in the US and the ensuing "global war on terror" — for leaders from ethnic, religious and community groups to communicate and meet regularly to build trust, and to organise community activities to deepen residents' understanding of various beliefs and practices. These groups — renamed Inter-Racial and Religious Confidence Circles in 2007 to also cover religious harmony — are established and active in every constituency.

Just "Majority Blind Spots", or Something More?

"Chinese privilege" and its variants

Day by day, serious hate crime is practically unheard-of in Singapore. But, more recently, some potentially unsettling forces appear to be afoot. While the island republic's openness to the world is undoubted, its ethnic cohesiveness at home has started to come under scrutiny amidst the stresses of pandemic times.

Since the emergence of Covid-19 in late 2019 and the partial lockdowns and other restrictions and disruptions from then on, there have been several incidents of what appeared to be racist actions on public transport and elsewhere in public. There were also episodes of racial insensitivity being called out, some making headlines on CNN and other international media, including a "brownface" advertisement, featuring a Chinese actor who darkened his skin to portray characters of different races.

The "last straw", as it were, was the incident along Orchard Road in June 2021 of a Chinese man (a polytechnic lecturer, later sacked because of this controversy) heckling a mixed-race couple – a half-Indian, half-Filipino man and his girlfriend, who is half-Singaporean Chinese, half-Thai – and telling them to date only within their own race.

These incidents prompted the government to act. In June 2021, Finance Minister Lawrence Wong stated the government's position on the issue, including a game-changing, unequivocal acknowledgement of the discrimination and stereotyping still experienced by ethnic minorities, and calling on the majority community to change, to "be sensitive to, and conscious of, the needs of minorities".

Then in August 2021, Prime Minister Lee Hsien Loong, at the National Day Rally, announced moves to establish new legislation for a Maintenance of Racial Harmony Act. In future, this law would, in all probability, come to do for racial harmony what the Maintenance of Religious Harmony Act has done for interfaith serenity, since it was enacted in 1990, complete with a Presidential Council for Religious Harmony.

Amidst the public discussions of a possible rise in racism, "Chinese privilege" is the most hotly debated term, which some see as being imported by those seeking to transplant ideas and perceptions from "woke culture" in the US. The loudest pushback to this charge has come from the Chinese-educated segment of the population, who have actually felt like a minority, despite their numbers, ever since English was made the main language of public life from the 1970s, leading to the closure in 1980 of Nanyang University, the highest-level institution in the Chinese education system.

If anything, from this angle, there is actually only "English-educated privilege", seen in the advantages of being part of the "establishment elite" who are fluent in English. This "English-educated privilege" can also exist in much humbler forms, such as for people like my late parents, who were Teochew and Hakka, but grew up as "British subjects" in colonial Singapore, effectively monolingual in English, and speaking hardly a word of Mandarin.

Overlaying this segmentation by language is the aspect of "inter-sectional ethnic privilege" – whereby members of any ethnic minority can also join the elite if they can attain the criteria for material success in society: being educated in English and having the requisite educational and professional qualifications, not to mention being linked to the most useful networks.

Just "Majority Blind Spots", or Something More?

This opens up the topic of the class divide, perhaps a subject for another book, titled *Regardless of Class*. What is pertinent here for advancing racial harmony is always to have an "intersectional mindset" about issues of race, as there are always other potentially divisive forces at play, including age, generational differences, gender, class, religion, socio-economic status, sexual orientation, and so on.

For members of minority communities, joining the societal elite lifts them above – and even completely out of – the situation still experienced by fellow members of their ethnic group. The power of real-life ethnic representation can be very visible, and Singapore has – what must seem to some observers – one of the most unexpected symbols of ethnic representation in an elected President who is a Malay/Muslim woman who wears a headscarf, in a country with a majority Chinese population.

More subtly, the power of ethnic representation in the media is regularly seen, for example, in the casting of an Indian family of doctors in the TV soap opera *Tanglin*, or two families of enterprising Malay and Eurasian business people in the series *Kin*.

In the recent discussions on racial harmony, some observers have revised the phenomenon in question from "majority privilege" to something less culpable: "majority blind spots", which are those aspects in life

> **Racial and religious differences might actually be mainly the symptoms – even the Trojan horses – of divisiveness. Instead, the real root causes of overt racism could be more bread-and-butter in nature, such as indignity and hopelessness.**

of discrimination and disadvantage that minorities have to live through, that members of the ethnic majority – Chinese in the case of Singapore – are blind to, because they have never had to endure such situations by virtue of their skin colour, an accident of birth.

For me personally, looking back, yes, there were certainly such instances of blindness, facets that I lacked the life experience and wisdom to be empathetic to, up to my teenaged years. But later in life, any such "majority blind spots" were removed, after some experiences of being reminded of my minority status. All the examples of such encounters that I am sharing in this book are from overseas – this is because I typically do not come across anything like this in Singapore, being from the majority ethnic group. This illustrates, very simply, what "privilege" means – the freedom to be yourself, to not be held back by any of the markers of your identity, including race.

Sometimes, being reminded of my minority status has happened with very innocent actions, such as my British college mate at Cambridge University in the UK in the 1980s mentioning, in one English literature tutorial, that the Chinese pictogram "管", a word used in a poem by the American writer Ezra Pound, looks a bit like Snoopy's kennel, in the comic strip *Peanuts*.

Less innocent interactions on my travels stripped away any of my remaining blinkers to the circumstances of ethnic minorities. After arriving as student backpackers in Finland in the early 1980s, my fellow Singaporean Chinese travel companion and I were stared at so much in the streets, from immigration and everywhere else we went (they probably thought we were from mainland China), that we felt so uncomfortable that we beat a hasty

Just "Majority Blind Spots", or Something More?

retreat and left on the next available ferry back to Sweden.

There was also this gypsy woman who spat at me, completely unprovoked (luckily she missed), when I was crossing a road, also backpacking in Europe, in a city that I cannot recall (as the Barbra Streisand song *The Way We Were* goes, "what's too painful to remember, we simply choose to forget…").

Pandemic effect? "Potholes" along the "road" of life

So today, if there is indeed a rise in racist sentiment, as the recent incidents seem to suggest, should Covid-19 shoulder part of the blame? Are there symptoms of "societal cabin fever"?

In June 2019, I attended the International Conference on Cohesive Societies (organised by the Rajaratnam School of International Studies with the support of the Ministry of Culture, Community and Youth). The speaker who left the deepest impression on me was Christian Picciolini, a former American neo-Nazi skinhead extremist in the US, who was later reformed, and broke away from white supremacist groups, to become the founder of the Free Radicals Project, a global network now working to prevent extremism, and to counsel and help people disengage from hate movements.

At the Singapore conference, Picciolini argued that race, religion, even identity, are all weapons used to sow discord. Of course, there would be pre-existing racial prejudices, but, invariably, what pushes people towards anti-social behaviour, actually acting out latent sentiments, are the "potholes" on the "roads" of their own lives. These are setbacks including family and societal neglect, disenfranchisement, and marginalisation. This effect would be magnified in the case of members of a majority community who feel hard done by, in the face of such "failures" caused by perceived injustices and unfairness in life. And if society then views them as "losers" – thereby adding the aspect of damage to self-esteem – this would only make the vicious circle even worse. Angst boils over into anger; prejudice into pre-meditated harm.

What this suggests is that racial and religious differences might actually be mainly the symptoms – sometimes, perhaps even the Trojan horses – of divisiveness in today's world. Instead, the real root causes of something like overt racism could be more bread-and-butter in nature, such as indignity and hopelessness, from perceived inequality, injustice and the lack, or loss, of economic opportunity. Just focusing on racism per se – as just primeval instinct that can be curbed by rationality – would then be barking up the wrong tree.

At the outset, what is seen as racism has always existed along a broad spectrum, ranging from plain, unthinking ignorance to pre-meditated, wilful hatred. At the lowest level, there will always be the "casual racism" that does not really hurt – that which is rooted in the "soil" of ingrained racial prejudice, much of it sub-conscious, which is then "watered" and "fertilised", learned from elders and peers in childhood, steeped in primordial tribal instinct, laced with ignorance. This becomes a kind of strange novelty with which ethnic minorities are viewed, that they are always destined to suffer. For example, pointing out odd physical features is somehow irresistible to some members of other races, such as Caucasians making slit-eye gestures to mock Asians, when hardly any Asian ever, say, mimics Caucasian hooked noses.

Just "Majority Blind Spots", or Something More?

This kind of childlike, sometimes childish, fascination probably accounts for the insatiable curiosity of the local Brazilian tourists sitting behind us in the boat ride that my wife and I took along the Amazon River in the 2010s. We could sense that they were discussing actively in Portuguese where we could be from, until one of them decided to ask us, to settle their own debate.

This would also explain the excitement of that young boy cycling in the streets of Havana, Cuba in the 2010s, who, upon seeing my wife and me strolling past, shouted "Chinas!" ("Chinese" in Spanish), alerting his pals to his sighting of this uncommon species in these here parts. The Singaporean equivalent would be young boys here, upon spotting a passing Caucasian person, calling out *"Ang moh lai liao!"* ("red-haired people coming!" in Hokkien), which they probably did up till the 1960s – surely a sign of a less civilised and cosmopolitan place, to say the least.

At the other end of the spectrum of racism, Picciolini's insight is that what turns latent prejudice into actual action is a motivation that comes from another source, such as someone of a majority race who has, say, lost a job or a girlfriend to an immigrant of another ethnicity, or, having lost out in some economic facet, feels envy, or even angst and anger, on seeing people of another race apparently doing better in life.

This might have prompted the young men on the street passing me and a relative I was visiting in Melbourne, Australia, in the 2010s, to make audible racist remarks mocking Chinese people – including some variation of "Chink", or something like that – as they walked by, as well as another group of young men who did the same, when I was strolling alone in Providence, Rhode Island, in the US in the 2000s.

If ignorance is at the root of it all – for example, a standing joke in the US is of white Americans who can call on just "one black friend" – the conditions that foment public racism are affected by what I call the "law of diminishing racial prejudice" – that is, if we tend to stereotype what we know less of, then, very simply, the more we know of people of another race, the less likely we are to think negatively of them.

This is why, if I were asked to give a proposal on what could be done to enhance racial harmony in Singapore, I would suggest that kindergartens, primary and secondary schools, and junior colleges and polytechnics, should invite more external speakers of diverse ethnicities to give talks to students; or at least, for teachers to screen videos of such speakers in class. These speakers could run the whole gamut of fields of life, from businesswomen to baristas, from politicians to poets.

In my time, I have given a few such talks, usually at a university or an institution like LASALLE College for the Arts, and have sometimes envied the students for being given the opportunity to tap the wisdom of lived experience of such speakers – something unheard-of in my own days at school and junior college in the 1970s and '80s. The resulting indirect benefit would be to racial harmony: The more we see people of other ethnicities speak well and show themselves as smart, successful and attractive – instead of lazy, untrustworthy, or just plain dumb – the more likely we would begin to jettison our own learned prejudices of them.

This might be why some people have observed that the younger generations seem, on balance, to be less racist, or more "race-blind" (if this is possible), than their seniors. The online universe – including movies and TV series on streaming services,

Just "Majority Blind Spots", or Something More?

YouTube, WhatsApp, the Internet in general – has presented many more positive visual images of people of other ethnicities. Of course, negative images abound as well, but the whole net effect could be less ignorance of other cultures, overall.

Hence, globally accessible media content – ranging from *Black Panther*, the first black Marvel superhero movie (2018), to *Squid Game*, the Korean Netflix series that took the world by storm in 2021 – can actually be helping to reduce racial prejudice, by subliminally opening more minds. If this is so, then having more real-life speakers of all ethnicities in class in Singapore's schools, acting as potential role models who might strike a formative chord, surely wouldn't hurt the cause of racial harmony.

With this and other adjustments, including those proposed by the 21 contributors to this book, perhaps, Singaporeans would then be able to move one more step forward together – in S. Rajaratnam's words – towards "forgetting" their ethnic differences, and "becoming" one united people.

Koh Buck Song is the author and editor of more than 30 books, including *Brand Singapore* (Marshall Cavendish, 2021, third edition, with a Chinese translation in China 2012) and *Around the World in 68 Days* (Penguin Random House SEA, 2021). As a journalist, columnist, and political, arts and world affairs supervisor at *The Straits Times* in the 1990s, many of his articles discussed racial harmony. As a country brand adviser, he often highlights multiculturalism as the X factor when speaking on brand Singapore, including in Bhutan, Japan, the UK, USA and Tahiti. As adjunct editor at the Centre for Liveable Cities, he has written on race relations as an aspect of urban liveability. He read English at Cambridge and has a master's in public administration from

Harvard. He was an adjunct professor in leadership at the Lee Kuan Yew School of Public Policy, and in media policy at Singapore Management University. Also a poet and *haiga* artist, he is the National Gallery Singapore's poet-in-residence 2021–22.

If We Start with Conversations, We Can Go Far

SALEEMAH ISMAIL

I was born in 1969, at the cusp of when changes were rife in a young Singapore. Singapore had just become independent, and with that came the uncertainties of the future.

Despite Singapore being a small country with no hinterland, I believe our potential was centred on our diverse multiracial society. Then, and even now.

The 1960s were a tumultuous period with a series of communal race-based disturbances between the Malays and Chinese in Singapore. A future with a fractured society was a real possibility, with everyone living in disquiet and mistrust of each other.

The riots and different ideologies of how to run a multiracial nation were among the factors that led to Singapore becoming independent, as Singapore hunkered down in its belief in a meritocratic society regardless of race, language, or religion.

Perhaps we would not be as racially integrated as we are today if we had not pursued the public policies that we did. Our housing and educational policies have been vital in the integration of the different races. The ethnic integration policy of the Housing & Development Board (HDB) played an enormous part because it removed ethnic enclaves, making it easier for all of us to integrate.

But perhaps the most effective policy was our education policy. Back then, there were a few social development programmes set up in schools, with the aim of encouraging integration not just across race and religion, but also social class. Wearing a school uniform is symbolic, as it helps to build the perception that everyone is equal in school, regardless of their social standing.

The bilingual policy also played a role in ensuring racial harmony. Decreeing that English be the lingua franca made sense – English was a language that was not "tied" to any one race, thus ensuring that no one race had a greater advantage over the others. It helped accord equality among the different races and ensure that no preferential treatment was given. It also encouraged communication between the different races. Practically, English was a tool that would help a young Singapore open up to the world and attract business.

I am privileged to have seen the transformation of Singapore from the fractured early days of public housing and education in the 1970s. From a country with no natural resources to the respected nation we are today, we have made great strides in racial harmony. We share common spaces and practise our religions freely. Telok Ayer Street is Singapore's representative street of religious harmony – home to a temple, a mosque and a church. I believe this is a rare sight not found in many parts of the world.

If We Start with Conversations, We Can Go Far

Making friends across racial, and other, differences

At New Life Stories, the non-profit organisation I co-founded in 2014, we like to think that we are doing our part, however small, in fostering interracial and religious friendships through our befriending programme. Volunteers from all age groups and backgrounds visit the homes of children of incarcerated parents. They read books, play games, and befriend these children to help them have a fairer start in life.

For example, we had five 14-year-old boys from a top, predominantly Chinese school who joined our fold as volunteers. They had no friends from a different race or socio-economic group, but wanted to reach out beyond their homogeneous circle while making a difference with children. We paired them with 8-year-old Yusuf. This was out of the ordinary, pairing five Chinese boys with a Malay child – organisations usually try to pair those of the same race together to reduce communication issues. But we believe that this difference is what made their bond unique.

It was not long before we saw Yusuf and the five boys embracing their friendship with open hearts and minds as they spent time in Yusuf's home every Saturday afternoon for over three years. Yusuf calls them *abang*, a Malay word for "elder brother". They have looked beyond skin colour to form a friendship, and remain Yusuf's befrienders till today.

The story of Yusuf and these boys is one of many. Despite the cultural, socio-economic and at times language barriers, we often hear heartwarming stories from both volunteers and families of the strong friendships that were forged. It is not uncommon for our volunteers to be called *abang* or *ge ge* ("elder brother" in Mandarin) by the children, or for them to be invited to family gatherings. Such is the impact of the close ties they forge together.

Through these house visits, racial stereotypes are debunked as well. Our volunteers had admitted that they had biases before they started. They believed in the stereotype, for instance, that Malay children are lazy or aren't goal-oriented. But through their friendships with the children, they started to realise that not everyone has the same start in life.

The children on our programme have many odds stacked against them. Many face multiple adverse childhood experiences – poverty, emotional and mental neglect, and abuse. It is unfair to judge these children, because their determination to improve their situation is always there, but they are hindered by circumstances such as economic stress and mental anguish – often even before they start primary school.

In turn, I see our volunteers feeling humbled by the hospitality and generosity of these families despite their low income. Sometimes, the families even prepare simple fare such as curry puffs and tea so that our volunteers can have a quick bite in-between sessions. While this may seem a small expense for most of us who are fortunate, to the families it is a cost that they fork out of the little that they have.

> **The learning experience goes two ways – the families and volunteers are proven wrong in their own stereotypes of other races. The families have told us they held preconceived notions that these sometimes-privileged volunteers would not be able to understand their plight, but they feel otherwise after these befriending sessions.**

If We Start with Conversations, We Can Go Far

We are glad that the learning experience goes two ways – the families and the volunteers are proven wrong in their stereotypes of other races. The families have told us they held preconceived notions that these sometimes-privileged volunteers would not be able to understand their plight and situation, but they felt otherwise after the befriending sessions.

What's due for review: CMIO and more
But, as we all know, the only constant in life is change. What has worked well in the past may not be relevant now. There have been many conversations recently about race, with Singaporeans discussing what it means to live in a multiracial society. With the proliferation of social media, it is so very easy to spread thoughts and ideas, whether correct or not – this is certainly up for debate.

In the beginning, the categorisation policy of CMIO (Chinese-Malay-Indian-Others) was necessary. It was effective, even, as it helped with ethnic integration and prevented enclaves. But is there still a need for it today? There have been so many interracial marriages. Racial lines are blurred. The generation now is also more accepting and understanding of other races and mix around on their own.

Perhaps it is now time for a review of such archaic categorisations. There has been discussion that the minorities bear a direct and real financial burden from the HDB ethnic integration policy.

The racially based self-help groups (Chinese Development Assistance Council, Eurasian Association, Singapore Indian Development Association and Yayasan MENDAKI) are also reminders of the CMIO categorisation. Wouldn't an income-based self-help group be much more effective, not only for collective self-help, but also to foster interracial cooperation and understanding?

Moving forward, Singapore's efforts in fostering racial harmony have to go beyond one day, i.e. Racial Harmony Day. More must be done. We need safe spaces to have open and honest dialogues about race all year round. It is what the younger generations now expect. Certain ground-up groups have shown that Singaporeans are ready and mature enough to talk about these issues.

Wouldn't an income-based self-help group be much more effective, not only for collective self-help, but also to foster interracial cooperation and understanding?

I also believe the best way to know someone is to have conversations in the person's home. When you go into someone's home every week for a year, you learn about their culture and way of life. You learn about their fears and dreams, you develop an understanding of each other, and you develop feelings for the person. As I would say, you don't like a person you don't understand. Just like how our volunteers examine their own biases and are proven wrong, perhaps we should normalise and scale such home visits. We need to have real conversations to bridge people of different tribes and vibes.

Only with conversations can there be understanding. Only with understanding can there be fellowship. Only with fellowship can there be feelings of love. And only with love can there be unity. So, the first step is conversations.

One united Singapore does not mean a homogeneous Singapore. A stronger Singapore is one where people of different tribes and vibes respect and help each other. I hope for the day when everyone in Singapore understands that diversity and inclusion make us stronger, not weaker. I hope for the day when every child gets a fair start in life, no matter the odds of their birth or early childhood. We are close to this day, but we must keep on trying, because in striving, we become a country of good.

Saleemah Ismail is a community activist, feminist and change-maker. She started her career in the private sector before moving to work for United Nations Women and the UN Development Programme in Asia and South America for over 15 years. She is the co-founder and Executive Director of New Life Stories, working with children of incarcerated parents, the incarcerated and their families to prevent intergenerational incarceration, reduce re-offending, improve quality of life and increase community inclusion for the families.

2

What We Must Do, to Begin to Talk About Racism

NAZRY BAHRAWI

2021 is the year that racism finally gets some serious public attention in Singapore. A series of outrageous racist outbursts in the middle of the year prodded some major policy changes by National Day, including the move to turn a set of anti-discrimination guidelines for the workplace into legislation, under the Tripartite Alliance for Fair and Progressive Employment Practices (TAFEP).

But, as the year comes to a close, there still appears to be little closure on how Singaporeans should move forward on the nation's shaky state of race relations.

At the moment, two overarching positions have emerged. On the one hand, the mainstream stance seems to take on a rationalist veneer. The narrative goes something like this: The pandemic and social media are largely to blame for some public racist episodes, but Singapore is still a multiracial safe space as long as its citizens do not try to unravel this. This is the cautionary view that dominates the mainstream media. It places the onus of change on individuals.

On the other hand, there are voices suggesting a less ideal story. Their position is that racism is more common, and more adverse, than we think. The pandemic and social media did not cause it but have, in fact, made it apparent. These voices can be loud, emotional and oftentimes firm. You can find these expressed on social networking sites as postings by individuals or community pages. To them, change cannot happen unless systems and structures are overhauled. It is high time that Singapore adopts new modes of thinking and doing things.

The two positions come to a head on the issue of "Chinese privilege". Within the rationalist camp, a number of commentators and politicians have dismissed it as unhelpful to racial discourse. In June 2021, this position was publicly voiced by the Chinese newspaper *Lianhe Zaobao* when it published an editorial condemning the use of Critical Race Theory (CRT) by some commentators to impose notions of "White privilege" onto "Chinese privilege", adding to unhappiness between racial groups.

Slightly more than a week later, an open letter signed by nearly 300 researchers and academics disagreed with *Zaobao*'s move to raise the spectre of insidious foreign ideologies. I was one of the letter's signatories because I concur with the letter's stance that "Westernisation" is a simplistic charge that feeds into the reductive theory of a civilisational clash between East and West.

Writing about this in an article for the website *Academia.SG* in July 2021, titled "A Vocabulary of Our Own", I have also posited that Singaporeans can do better with engaging scholarship that is closer to home in pursuit of developing our own critical vocabulary on race. This is one way we can break the impasse on our racial discourse.

However, the public uptake of such a move will require time even if smatterings of local scholarship on race exist. For instance, scholars need to engage and critique concepts and positions between themselves, a process that might take years, even decades. Then, there is the matter of the public's acceptance or dismissal of some of these ideas and concepts.

Covert parallels and emotional depth in the experience of racism

What can we do in the meantime?

I would posit three proposals as a scholar of comparative literature, a field that deals with affinities and disjunctures of texts, thoughts and traditions between cultures.

It is often said that one should only compare apples to apples. I have discovered in my study that one can compare apples to oranges for the fact that they are both fruits. In other words, parallels exist in seemingly disparate phenomena if we look closely enough. My first proposal is that covert parallels matter as much as overt ties. How do we apply this to racism?

Drawing parallels between "blackface" and "brownface", while acknowledging their cultural differences, would offer clues to Chinese Singaporeans about younger Singaporeans' chastisement of the episode.

While details differ, the experience of racism is universal, whether a person is an African-American, or an Indian or Malay

Singaporean. For Singapore's ethnic minorities, subjected to years of culturally insensitive advertisements, the term "brownface" is not a foreign ideology imposed on us. Quite the opposite. "Brownface" represents access to a critical vocabulary that can help us express the racism we face as a lived reality in the absence of our own cultural register.

The strong reaction that came from members of the ethnic minority community to the use of "brownface" for an e-Nets advertisement in 2019, especially from younger Singaporeans, may have taken a number of Chinese Singaporeans by surprise. Drawing parallels between "blackface" and "brownface", while acknowledging their cultural differences, would offer clues to Chinese Singaporeans about younger Singaporeans' chastisement of the episode.

A second suggestion builds on another kind of acknowledgment: the idea that emotions are significant. This is especially important when dealing with the trauma of racism as a qualitative experience. A person who has experienced racism is seldom listless about it, even if that person does not show it. Their rage, frustration, despair and much more mark their social media posts. Emotional depth is also a feature of many literary narratives that deal with racial inequalities, such as August Wilson's play *Fences* (1985), which was adapted into a 2016 film directed by Denzel Washington. For the racial discourse to move forward in Singapore, it would do us well not to dismiss such impassioned reactions.

Often, feelings have been invalidated through data and surveys, some of which are referenced as proof of Singapore's healthy state of race relations. Indeed, surveys, when properly done, could really help us tackle racism. But, have we tabulated the data right?

Not quite, according to the sociologist Shannon Ang in an article in July 2021 for *Academia.SG*, titled "Race-Based Data: Friend or Foe?". Among his proposals is the need to contextualise race-based data with more data to present a more accurate picture of what is happening on the ground.

As an experience and a moral issue, racism must surely be approached from the perspectives of ethics, structures and narratives. Instead of over-relying on a "big data" study of racism, Singapore should consider embarking on a qualitative, even philosophical, approach to it. This means asking the right questions even before attempting to tabulate. Here, the question I think we should be asking ourselves is "How can we tackle racism in Singapore?" and not "Does racism exist in Singapore?" or "Is brownface relevant to Singapore?". This would expedite the development of a contextually relevant critical vocabulary on race in Singapore.

Managing thought leadership in a "post-racialised society"

My final suggestion concerns the management of thought leadership on race. A number of commentators have emerged as the go-to voices in the mainstream media on race, mediating the racial discourse, herding Singaporeans towards certain perspectives on the matter. One such position is the dismissal of "Chinese privilege" as a concept. My counter-view to this is that the concept presents Singaporeans with the opportunity to speak frankly about ethnic relations from the perspective of structures and systems.

Another concept that has gained currency is the ideal of the "post-racial society". To me, a better ideal to pursue is the "post-racialised society". The former suggests that race does not matter in a society, and that we can be colour-blind, so to speak. This dismisses the rich traditions and lived experiences of people of different races, cultures and civilisations. It flattens and disregards the superdiversity in our world. The latter is an ideal that we can get behind because it recognises that there is value in acknowledging our different ethnic and cultural backgrounds. It also posits that we should not make race our primary identity marker that dictates the way we make policies and laws. It also means we must tackle racial discrimination.

> A better ideal to pursue is the "post-racialised society"... we should not just make race our primary identity marker that dictates the way we make policies and laws.

In the spirit of diversity, it is also time for Singapore to listen to thought leaders beyond these go-to voices. Some of these can be found on social media in the form of community pages like Minority Voices. Others include the Anti-Racism Coalition (Singapore), which was part of a group of civil society groups that submitted shadow reports on racial discrimination to the United Nation's Committee on the Elimination of Racial Discrimination in November 2021. Then, there are individuals like Sarah Bagharib, who has emerged as a courageous voice against racial discrimination following the misuse of her wedding photograph as part of a Hari Raya Aidilfitri standee put up by the People's Association.

The Chinese writer Lu Xun's short story *Diary of a Madman* (1918) ends with its protagonist pleading to "save the children" from the cannibalistic norms of his village, a metaphorical message about the perils of stubbornly maintaining the status quo. I would like to end this piece to the contrary of that: a hopeful message that it is some of Singapore's young who can save its older folks from the scourge of racism, despite the latter's insistence on talking over and educating them. We can do better.

Nazry Bahrawi is an assistant professor of Southeast Asian literature and culture at the University of Washington in the US. He is also the editor-at-large of *Wasafiri* magazine and the editor (essay and research) at the *Practice, Research and Tangential Activities (PR&TA)* journal.

3

Can Singapore's Multiculturalism Return to Its Best Days?

MATILDA GABRIELPILLAI

It's often assumed that race relations in Singapore have been improving since nationhood. The racial riots of the 1950s and '60s loom large in the Singapore imagination, creating a "founding myth" that, with independence, we Singaporeans escaped from the fires of racial hatred of our Malayan days. It's believed that we have been on an upward trajectory of interracial harmony since.

However, I remember the late 1950s, '60s and "nation-building" years of the '70s quite differently – as the halcyon days of Singapore's multiculturalism, to which we have yet to return.

The heady cultural hybridity of the 1950s–'70s
My first home in the late 1950s was at my grandparents' house in a Malay rural section of the East Coast, just next door to a mosque, and later in the Naval Base at Sembawang, where Indians were

the majority but boasted an easy, even intimate, camaraderie with their Chinese and Malay neighbours.

My grandparents had migrated to Singapore from Sri Lanka in the 1910s but, 40 years later, Malay and Western music would emanate from their phonograph, thanks to my hip uncles and youngest aunt. English and Tamil were spoken most frequently at home, but my grandmother and I would often converse in a mix of English and Malay, as my Tamil was below par and she spoke minimal English. By the 1970s, one uncle had married a Malay woman, and the other, a Chinese one. My swinging aunt, who had the most colourful mix of church friends, married into a Sri Lankan Malaysian family that would always strike me as being more Eurasian than Tamil in their culture.

These were the days before the British pullout from Singapore, when English culture was part and parcel of the heady cultural hybridity of those days. My English next-door neighbour in Sembawang Hills Estate, where I lived till I was eight, was Eileen, paradoxically both exotic and familiar to me, culturally different from me but behaving just like a character from one of my favourite Enid Blyton books. She would break off our daily evening conversations across the fence when her mother called her in to have cookies and milk before going to bed at 8 p.m.

I slept at 10 p.m., having had dinner just an hour before (something that many Tamil families still do). The mobile food businesses that serviced our estate then included the *mee goreng*, *satay* and *tau huay* hawkers who would come by on their push-carts, as well as the fish-and-chips trucks with their dimly lit interiors that beamed mystery and magic into the estate on their nightly rounds.

My pre-teen years took me to another cultural universe, the

Can Singapore's Multiculturalism Return to Its Best Days?

SIT (Singapore Improvement Trust) flats from colonial times in Queenstown, which featured an even more intense diversity. At home, my father, who was a popular English Literature teacher then, would hold court in our living room with his secondary school students, explicating Shakespearean moral ideologies about honour and integrity and the importance of reputation, while I kicked about the playground with vernacular-educated and English-educated Indian and Chinese kids.

Mondays to Fridays, I devoured the novels by Charles Dickens, Thomas Hardy and George Eliot that sat in my father's antique bookcase, while the weekends were reserved for Bharata Natyam dance classes and socialising with friends and family at the Ceylon Tamils' Association or catching Tamil movies at the Diamond Theatre on North Bridge Road.

Musically, I moved between Hokkien songs sung at *getai* performances on makeshift stages set up opposite my block, Cliff Richard and Engelbert Humperdinck as well as local groups like Naomi and the Boys played in the home of the Eurasian family upstairs, and Anneke Gronloh, Julie Sudiro and Kartina Dahari at my grandparents' place.

The late 1950s, '60s and "nation-building" years of the '70s were the halcyon days of Singapore's multiculturalism, to which we have yet to return.

At school, I never felt any race-consciousness at the Catholic mission school I attended for 10 years, despite being a dark-skinned Indian, a contrast to my cousin's children who would be ragged 30 years later for their names and skin colour in the 1990s. The only racism I observed around me then was with some

Chinese shopkeepers who would keep their cash-paying local customers waiting while waiting hand-and-foot on their British Forces clientele, who often left for England without paying their extensive grocery bills.

In fact, I did not experience the local Chinese population as a "race" until the 1980s and '90s. At hawker stalls, my Chinese friends would receive the same treatment as me, because the stallholder, being of a different dialect group from my friends, would treat all of us as equally alien to him. On the other hand, an Indian friend who was fluent in most of the Chinese dialects could twirl Chinese stallholders around her little finger, getting us extras and freebies because she could chat nineteen to the dozen with them in their dialect.

The real impact of a "Chinese cultural elite"
The days when interracial groups of friends were a common sight at school, university and residential estates began to change with the "Speak Mandarin" campaign of the early 1980s. Although done with an economic purpose in mind – to equip Singaporeans with the language skills required to take advantage of China's opening its doors to business – the Speak Mandarin campaign and the clamping down of dialects unified the local Chinese, homogenising them into a race, erasing their dialectal diversity in one fell swoop.

Over the decade, this would turn out to be a step in developing a racialised mode of governance. Inspired by two books by American thinker Herman Kahn in 1979 that advanced the theory that the "tiger economies", including Singapore, had managed their quick rise to prosperity due to their supposed "Confucianist" ethos, the Singapore government would pour much investment into promoting Confucianism in the country. A new Religious Knowledge programme was put in place, and American Sinologists were invited to help set up the Institute of East Asian Philosophies. If Confucianism had indeed been a crucial part of the Singapore success story, then it was baffling that its DNA could not be found in our local intellectual fabric.

Recently, there has been a lot of gnashing of teeth at the notion that there is such a thing as "Chinese privilege" on our shores. Tongues have wagged at the terrible fate the Chinese-educated had suffered in our nation-building years, economically and culturally displaced with the removal of Chinese-stream schools and the closure of Nanyang University in 1980.

But people forget that the other vernacular stream schools were also closed. Now, imagine the thoughts and feelings of Indian, Malay and Eurasian youth and working adults, as they heard the daily calls from ministers in the 1980s to form a "Chinese cultural elite" and to set up Special Assistance Plan schools to produce this English-Mandarin bicultural elite. This is the story of minority disenfranchisement that has yet to be told.

> **Imagine the thoughts and feelings of Indian, Malay and Eurasian youth and working adults, as they heard daily calls from ministers in the 1980s to form a "Chinese cultural elite" and set up Special Assistance Plan schools to produce this English-Mandarin bicultural elite. This is the story of minority disenfranchisement that has yet to be told.**

Words hurt. But words spoken by national leaders on the national stage can be even more cutting. The words "Chinese cultural elite" were more hurtful to me than being called a "black face". It meant there was a glass ceiling over my head.

I come from a generation that was inspired by our first Prime Minister's vision of a multicultural nation. Lee Kuan Yew would speculate hopefully in the 1960s and '70s that "over the centuries something distinctive may emerge [in Singapore culture], something different from China or India or Indonesia or Britain". He would also speak of "an ethnic assimilation or cultural homogeneity blurring out the cultural boundaries now co-existing". In a speech delivered soon after Singapore attained independence but long-forgotten now, Mr Lee showed utmost, touching concern for minority communities, stating:

> The problem was how to create a situation where the minority, either in ethnic, linguistic or religious terms, was not conscious that it was a minority, and that the exercise of its rights as equal citizens with all others was so natural and so accepted by society that it was not conscious of the fact that it was sharing equal rights with the others in dominant ethnic groups.

Why wouldn't a young minority woman like me – who had kept pace with Lee's dreams of a race-blind Singapore, who had seen him shed tears over national TV over the defeat of a wonderfully progressive ideal of a "Malayan Malaya" – feel betrayed by changed policies that would always remind Singaporeans of their race, of their dominant or minority status? Policies such as the Ethnic Integration Policy for public housing, the Group Representation Constituency scheme of ensuring that minorities are politically represented, the Mother Tongue policy, the racialised self-help groups. I watched crestfallen as the main metaphor for our distinct Singaporean culture changed from that of a "melting pot" to that of a "mosaic", from cultural fusion to racial separation.

National ideology and "other-ing"

The situation would get worse for minority groups. In 1987, two right-wing American ideologues, Ezra Vogel and George Lodge, published the book *Ideology and National Competitiveness: An Analysis of Nine Countries*, that would take Kahn's ideas further by linking the "Confucianist" ethos of East Asian societies to a "national ideology" that could produce a "communitarian democracy", a euphemism for a political system that could negate "troublesome" human rights in service of the chase for money. The two writers theorised that the greater the ideological coherence of a nation, the better would be its economic performance.

Then-First Deputy Prime Minister Goh Chok Tong, waiting in the wings in 1988 to take on the helm of government from Lee Kuan Yew, announced that his first project would be to formulate a "national ideology", even acknowledging his indebtedness to the Vogel and Lodge book. Although promoted as a "quest" for shared values, the political values of "society before self" and "consensus rather than contention" were announced before the various communities were consulted. Mr Goh, speaking of the SAP schools, said that this would ensure that "the people at the top are proficient in Chinese and possess the strong virtues of Chinese society" so that "they will give Singapore its Asian ballast".

Thus the "Asianising" of Singapore by the government was also simultaneously its "Sinicising".

Since the "National Ideology" values were never enacted in Parliament, the project appeared to have failed in ideologising the population. However, an incident occurred three years later, in 1994, to suture the so-called "shared values" into citizens' minds as part of our national identity. During the infamous Michael Fay caning episode, the Singapore government took the opportunity to oppose American liberal ideas of crime and punishment and the culture of individualism as being inimical to our "Asian values". Against a seeming threat to local sovereignty posed by President Bill Clinton's appeal against teenager Fay's caning sentence of six *rotan* strokes for theft and vandalising 18 cars, the public and media responded by identifying heartily with "Asian values" and investing this nationalist rhetoric with desire.

When I started teaching at a local university in 2000, Singaporean Chinese students would often talk confidently about their Asian values and identity, but be unable to explicate how this corresponded with their own lifestyles and values, suggesting their uncritical internalising of the rhetoric.

There is much cynicism now among humanities scholars about the intellectual credibility of totalising divergent Asian cultures as one. As the "National Ideology" project showed, such a production required one culture to be used as a base, and any contrary and crucial aspects of other cultures to be erased or forgotten in the imagining of this new "nativist" Asian nationalism. Philip Jeyaretnam's novel *Abraham's Promise* offers an understanding of important aspects of local South Asian intellectual heritage that had to be excised by this insistence on our "Confucianist" heritage.

Can Singapore's Multiculturalism Return to Its Best Days?

National identity, founded on ideology in some form, has always involved excluding and including people and cultures, with geographical national boundaries being the most active sites of "other-ing". In cosmopolitan Singapore, the "other-ing" turns mostly on internal elements of race. This lack of recognition of minority communities as being just as Singaporean can be seen implicitly as well as explicitly: in the relative invisibility of minority communities in English-language advertisements and television shows, and as newsmakers in the media, as well as in violence enacted against the minorities and verbal bullying. In academia, attention was given unreflexively to the cultural heritage of the majority race.

It is ironic that concern for the deficient "cultural ballast" of Singaporeans was cited as the reason for our Mother Tongue policy. Our younger, more bilingual generations have certainly been able to access their formal cultural heritage better than the older, English-educated generations. However, it has not meant cultural confidence for the minority communities. They are daily made to feel "other" to the norm, and often entertain self-doubt about their place in the nation. They bear silently with ignored job applications or being passed over for promotions (often with their "difference" cited as the reason they didn't qualify). Without strong unionism and poor oversight of management, still others have quietly lost their jobs or seen their careers terminated because of the colour of their skin.

It is time that the government recognises it has a contractual obligation to ensure equal opportunities and equal visibility for the minority races in this multiracial Southeast Asian nation. But the proposed anti-racism legislation that does not involve fines or jail terms for offenders only tells a story of political leaders who don't think causing racial injury to fellow citizens — depriving them of opportunities to prosper, debilitating them psychologically, using one's authority to mock their culture — is a crime in the way that, say, shoplifting is.

Given the situation, minorities and anti-racism activists have an educational, consciousness-raising job on their hands. You should shout from the rooftops every time you or other people are racially discriminated at the workplace. Publicise it, demand answers from management; write about your hurt, your family's sorrow at being sidelined; criticise false knowledge and untrue claims about racism in Singapore. Don't let the majority community draw up the parameters for definitions of racism — you should do it, because you are the expert, only you have first-hand knowledge of it. Produce art, literature, academic knowledge on minority communities. Collect evidence. Produce evidence. Don't let anyone get away with telling you that you are imagining racism. Without transgressing boundaries set by laws, there is still plenty you can do.

Dr Matilda Gabrielpillai was a journalist with newspapers and magazines before pursuing a career as an academic and teacher-trainer in Singapore. With a PhD from the University of British Columbia and other post-graduate training in literature and the arts, she researched and taught cultural theory, post-colonial literatures and women's writing. Nationalisms and the scripting of cosmopolitan identities, as well as race and gender issues, were her favourite concerns. Currently, she is a freelance writer and tutor of English literature. She also runs a literature education website (www.literaturehelpdesksg.com) providing resources for students in local and international literature programmes.

4

A Reset Needed for Racial Harmony

BRAEMA MATHIAPARANAM

The beginnings of diversity, from old Singapura
The history of Singapura is often cited as having begun in 1819 when the British Empire's Sir Stamford Raffles "founded" it. But earlier records, some dating back to the 13th century, show that a mix of people – Orang Asli, Bugis, Javanese, Sumatrans, Chinese, South Asians, Jews, Arabs, British, Dutch, French and others – were residents and visitors living off the land and the sea, as a community, at various times over the past seven centuries. Singapura was born through easy access, an island nestled at the southern tip of the Malay Peninsula.

Sri Tri Buana (also known as Sang Nila Utama) of Palembang, who came to rule over Temasek, as the island was known then, chose to call it Singapura. This kingdom ended when the last king fled to Malacca to escape a scandal and the Majapahit forces who were already in Sumatra and Java. What is pertinent here is Singapore's longstanding plurality – a diverse people living in a regional, cultural, ethnic, religious, porous community.

Over time, more people came to find their keep. The British, too, brought more people from other colonised countries. By 1897, there were 200,000 people in Singapore. Women came to support husbands or to find work. Those who spoke English, or were educated in English, were given better jobs. People lived in racial clusters, a common practice with migrant populations, for easy support and comfort from within. The priority was to eke out a living, become successful, resettle in Singapore and live in kinship with each other and with others outside the tribe. This was the canvas to keep a livelihood, achieve success and be at peace.

The formation of multiracialism
World War II upset this balance. With some people already resenting being colonised, the war deepened the desire for self-rule and independence, as no one would wish to be owned or conquered. WWII showed how hate and ill-will had decimated millions of Jews in Europe and Chinese in Asia as the Nazis and Japanese, respectively, targeted these two groups, relentlessly. Passionate leaders of different origins, jobs, education levels and class emerged, focused on shaping an independent Malaya. The race-religion-culture vein also took on a fervour, and conflicts emerged, resulting in three racial riots that hit a nerve.

The first in 1950 were the Maria Hertogh race riots, which showed many factors at play: a Dutch-Catholic girl who grew up Muslim in her adoptive family was returned, against her will, by court order to her Catholic parents in the Netherlands; media images of Maria praying before statues of Christ and Mary irked many Muslims; her Muslim parents' love and hospitality were rebuffed when they had embraced her as their own; and a judiciary of colonisers. But the media and the people saw only the difference in race and religion. People died and were injured in the riots as tensions also grew in neighbouring Indonesia.

The second riot, in July 1964, broke out as political and community leaders fanned the race card knowing that tens of thousands of people would gather to observe the Prophet Mohammed's birthday. Malaysia's main political party, the United Malays National Organisation (UMNO), was advocating for privileges for Malays as *bumiputeras* (sons of the soil) whilst Singapore's People's Action Party (PAP) was intent on a non-communal, united approach for all people. Strategic communications through speeches, leaflets and rumour-mills galvanised many Malays in Malaysia and Singapore into targeting the Chinese, fearing they would take away their land, livelihoods, religion and culture. People were killed and injured; places destroyed.

The third racial riot was post-Independence, in 1969, after Malaysia's General Elections, when Sino-Malay confrontations spilled over into three months, resulting in deaths, injuries and destruction of property.

These severe frictions led Singapore's political and community leaders to focus, principally, on preventing the deepening of racial and religious divides. Founding Prime Minister Lee Kuan Yew promised in 1965, on Singapore's National Day (9 August): "This is not a Malay nation; this is not a Chinese nation; this is not an Indian nation. Everyone will have his place, equal: language, culture, religion." This was an expedient move, as Singapore was located in the centre of the then newly independent countries of Indonesia and Malaysia, which were focused on establishing privileges for Indonesian- and Malaysian-Muslims, whereas Singapore's majority was Chinese, with an indigenous Malay-Muslim population.

Hence, the PAP accorded the Malay community special provisions enshrined in the Singapore Constitution. The new government described it as its responsibility and in its interest to uphold this provision and that of Article 12(1), which states that "all persons are equal before the law and entitled to the equal protection of the law", unless exceptions are specified by government as given in Article 12(2) and (3). Based on Article 153, the Administration of the Muslim Law Act was enacted, and MUIS (Majlis Ugama Islam Singapore) and the Syariah Court were established for Muslims to be governed by Islamic law on personal matters of marriage, divorce, inheritance and guardianship. The community was given free tertiary education till 1989, when means-testing was introduced as more Malays had risen into higher income brackets.

Other policies to build up equality and cohesion amongst Singaporeans include:

- Making English in 1966 the lingua franca. Malay, Mandarin and Tamil became second languages, later identified as Mother Tongue Languages (MTL).
- Establishing the Presidential Council for Minority Rights in 1970 to scrutinise laws to ensure that no discrimination takes place against any ethnic minority group.
- Creating the Group Representation Constituency (GRC) system in 1988 so that Parliament would always have minority representation, as political parties had

to field at least one minority candidate in each GRC of three to six candidates.
- Introducing in 1989 the Ethnic Integration Policy (EIP) that mandates a quota on public housing flats to be bought by minorities, to prevent racial enclaves from forming in public housing estates.
- Setting up in the 1980s Mendaki as a self-help group, as Malay community leaders were concerned that Malay students were lagging behind in education. In the 1990s, other ethnic-based self-help groups were formed – the Singapore Indian Development Association (Sinda), the Chinese Development Assistance Council (CDAC) and the Eurasian Association.
- Launching Racial Harmony Day on 21 July 1997 to remember the riots and teach students the importance of maintaining racial and religious harmony in Singapore's multicultural and multi-ethnic society. It is now part of the National Education programme for schools. Racial Harmony Day is also a community event now organised by grassroots organisations led by People's Association, Community Development Councils (CDCs) and the civic society organisation OnePeople.sg. There is also an Orange Ribbon to commemorate racial harmony.
- Having in 1979 the Special Assistance Plan (SAP), whereby Chinese students are immersed in school in an environment of Chinese culture, history and language, to become effectively bilingual. When responding to feedback on the lack of such provisions for Malays and Indians, the Ministry of Education reiterated that SAP

schools are part of "Singapore's approach for every community to preserve and practise their cultures, religion and languages, while safeguarding the common space to develop a distinctive Singaporean identity", adding that Malay and Tamil language learners, "whose population is smaller" had an Elective Programme in Malay Language for Secondary Schools and the National Elective Tamil Language Programme.

- Setting up the Tripartite Alliance for Fair and Progressive Employment Practices (TAFEP) in 2006, to promote the adoption of fair, responsible and progressive employment practices. Its role is to advise both employers and employees, and alert the Ministry of Manpower to employers' unfair practices. In August 2021, TAFEP was strengthened to act legally against employers who have been unfair to workers. This is something long overdue, as almost each day there is an official complaint – between 2014 and 2021, TAFEP received an average of 379 workplace discrimination complaints each year.

The real fear of having a divisive Singapore and dealing with racial riots propelled many of the policies discussed above.

The effects of mother tongue, housing quota and other policies

Has the original purpose of equality and building a cohesive society been achieved through the above-mentioned policies? I discuss some of them here.

The Mother Tongue Languages (MTL) policy has caused much distress and disruption. In 1966, MT became an examinable subject to gain entry into secondary school, and in 1979, to gain a spot at university. This meant that students' education journey could be curtailed if they failed to do well in MT, causing much stress as education is key to success in Singapore.

The MTL gave no options in choices – Mandarin for Chinese students, Malay for Malay students and Tamil for all Indian students. In the early years, Tamil was not available and I, as a Ceylonese Tamil by race on my identity card, studied Malay. Despite concerns raised, many Indian students struggled with Malay, and in some cases Tamil (Tamil is not a mother tongue for all Indians), before five other Indian languages – Bengali, Gujarati, Hindi, Punjabi and Urdu – were included. Non-Chinese students also found it difficult to opt to study Mandarin, which has an economic quotient, as a second language.

> Over the years, Mandarin has become a lingua franca alongside English... when the majority of Chinese speak to each other in Mandarin, leaving out Malays and Indians in the classroom, at the workplace, in social gatherings and even in adult training centres.

This emphasis on MTL has also disrupted inter-generational interactions, as much of the ability to speak in dialects or in the Malay-dialects-English patois of Peranakan Chinese has been lost, and not everyone in the older Chinese generations can speak Mandarin well. Some bright students with poor MT scores went into the Normal Stream meant for slower-paced learning processes.

"Overuse" of Singlish was also deemed to have impacted the quality of Singaporeans' English. In 2000, the government introduced the Speak Good English Movement, to reinforce English as a common neutral language across the races. However, over the years, Mandarin has become a lingua franca alongside English, with many Chinese speaking to each other in Mandarin, leaving out Malays and Indians in the classroom, at the workplace, in social gatherings and even in adult training centres. Resentment is building up over this. This phenomenon of Mandarin as a main language of communication is also possibly aligning with Chinese ethnic pride in the wake of China's global rise.

Having four race-based self-help groups instead of one large organisation with multiple community locations means a duplication of human and financial resources. It also reinforces, psychologically, materially and socially, that help ought to come from within one's own race. The government insists that having four race-based self-help groups is better, as certain community problems are better dealt with from within these communities. Yet, countries such as Britain, Australia and Thailand with their diverse communities have hybrid structures of national services, with community or faith-based services to call upon when needed.

The EIP policy, which makes assumptions on minority behaviours being potentially threatening, affects those applying for public housing, where prices have escalated steeply beyond parallel increases in median incomes. Thus, first-time buyers of units on the Home Ownership Scheme worry about costs and queue position, and that some units are unavailable as they are reserved for minority buyers, who also face limited choices.

By contrast, private condominiums and landed properties

do not have minority-based quotas, which means that minorities can create enclaves if they so wish. This has already happened, as many foreigners on work visas buy homes or rent properties in locations where people from the same country of origin reside.

Race is also politicised, as the GRC scheme focuses on having a minority MP candidate in the GRC team. Yet, in past general elections and by-elections, minority candidates in single-seat constituencies have been chosen by the electorate over Chinese candidates. But the scheme has certainly also made it harder for opposition parties to find enough candidates to contest in all the GRCs.

On three occasions, leaders of Singapore have expressed reservations over having an Indian as Prime Minister. In the 1980s, founding Prime Minister Lee Kuan Yew said he had considered then-Minister for National Development, S. Dhanabalan, for the role, but decided that the country was "not ready" for an Indian head of government. In 2008, Prime Minister Lee Hsien Loong echoed his father's views, shortly after Barack Obama became the first black president of the United States, saying, when asked about Singapore's next Prime Minister: "Will it happen soon? I don't think so, because you have to win votes. And these sentiments – who votes for whom, and what makes him identify with that person – these are sentiments which will not disappear completely for a long time, even if people do not talk about it, even if people wish they did not feel it." Yet, the PM reiterated the need to have a non-Chinese President as that person is a "unifying symbol" of multiracial Singapore. Then-Deputy Prime Minister Heng Swee Keat had also said that older Singaporeans were not ready for a non-Chinese PM.

Procedurally, the people of Singapore do not vote in a Prime Minister. It is the ruling political party that chooses its leader, who then becomes the leader of the country. In 2018, the opposition Workers' Party had a renewal of leadership, choosing a non-Chinese, Pritam Singh, as its Secretary-General, who is now also the Leader of the Opposition in Parliament. These questions arise often as many Singaporeans view Senior Minister Tharman Shanmugaratnam to be highly capable, having held top leadership positions in Singapore and internationally; he is also popular with the people, scoring the highest winning margins with his GRC team in the last two general elections. Despite the merits of a non-Chinese and the strength of election polls, the PAP's decision-making process on the future premiership is pitched differently even as elected members continue to make speeches on equality and non-discrimination.

More people are using social media more frequently. In 2020, more than 88%, or 4.7 million of Singapore's population of 5.45 million, were using the Internet. The most popular social media platforms were YouTube, WhatsApp and Facebook for more than four out of five people. Young social media users here flock to Instagram, Snapchat and TikTok. There is rapid penetration of news, mis- and dis-information, which laws could be used to counter the adverse effects of, including the Protection from Online Falsehoods and Manipulation Act (POFMA), Penal Code, Internal Security Act, the about-to-be-implemented Foreign Interference Countermeasures Act (FICA), Defamation Act, and Maintenance of Religious Harmony Act.

In Singapore, the dissatisfaction over how CECA (the India-Singapore Comprehensive Economic Cooperation

Agreement) has allowed "too many" Indians to be employed in mid-career jobs in the information technology and finance industries has led to an abundance of racist vitriol online. This has clouded the lack of transparency over employment processes or redress procedures. There are almost a million foreign workers on work passes, many in healthcare, construction, service and domestic work. But digitalisation, changing work skills, the pandemic, and loss of jobs have exacerbated Singaporeans' insecurity, probably leading to racism against Indians.

There are 3.5 million Singaporeans amongst the 5.45 million persons in Singapore. Almost a third of marriages are transnational and one in five marriages are inter-ethnic. So, it brings into sharp focus the relevancy of the CMIO (Chinese, Malay, Indian, Others) model of framing the racial composition in Singapore. The CMIO model is outdated, and, more importantly in a globalised world, outmoded. Racial groups are becoming a conglomerate of different races, ethnicities and cultures.

> **As it was in the beginning when it was Temasek, and people depended on each other and formed bonds of friendship and respect, it is crucial now that globalised and highly digitised Singapore makes drastic changes to recalibrate its value code on unabridged compliance to equality for the people.**

I myself am a Ceylonese Tamil by race, coming under "Others" as I am not an Indian but my mother was given a race identity of "Indian". Children born to parents of two different races are a blend of identities. Singapore accepts between 15,000 and 25,000 new citizens a year from various countries. Data is not transparent – ethnicity and country of origin are not in the public domain. Yet, the racial demographic profiling remains consistently around 76% Chinese, 15% Malays, 7.5% Indians and 1.5% Others. So, what are the criteria used to assess who deserves to become a Singapore citizen? How are these CMIO proportionalities maintained? Befuddling.

The work ahead
Singapore is hard-pushed to maintain the CMIO model, as the identities of people go beyond just race: they are Singaporeans and also embrace a blend of cultures. We need to harness our internal value code of equality, fairness and integrity. So, here are some measures I am suggesting, most of which, sadly, are not new:

- Reconfigure a value code of equality, which means no special position, no discrimination, for any person, but instead, a certainty of provisions to fulfil people's needs. Because of digitalisation, Singapore's changing demographics, and an increase in conflicts worldwide, our code of values should be recentred on the first principles of equality and dignity for each person on our soil, regardless of race, religion, gender, socio-economic class, education, etc.
- Deconstruct what "racism" means, accepting that racism exists in cultural and institutional forms; not seeing racism as personal prejudices but more introspectively to realise how pervasive it is within the system, especially whenever there is a vast majority of one race which

rarely admits to racism as often there are vested interests in safeguarding privilege.
- Review the outmoded CMIO model and the GRC which is hollowly premised on race-requirements.
- Endorse English as the only lingua franca.
- Endorse an environment of integrity, honesty, transparency and clarity on policies, rules and processes so that they are inclusive of all persons, to reach national outcomes.
- Review and amend the policies mentioned above so that they are framed to achieve inclusivity and diversity of all persons.
- Draft the Racial Harmony Act – or is it not better to call it the Racial Equality Act – so as to eliminate racism and address prejudices, with clear criteria for mediation, education and punitive measures.
- Enact an Anti-Discrimination Act so that it covers discriminatory behaviour and acts beyond just the workplace as it does under TAFEP.
- Organise as a norm more interactive activities amongst all people in Singapore, including migrant workers on the core principles of equality, inclusivity and diversity.
- Review education programmes for children and introduce training programmes for adults in racism, discrimination, equality, inclusivity and diversity that address concepts of: "marginalisation"; "patronising"; "stereotyping people by their race"; "tolerance"; "conflicts, disagreements"; "addressing discrimination when

it happens"; "bystander"; "being blind"; "direct discrimination"; "indirect discrimination"; "harassment"; "victimisation negotiation"; "humanity"; "blaming the victim"; etc.
- Establish good practices with transparency and clear standards for occupational requirements placed in advertisements of job vacancies.
- Ensure that all career clinics for students about to enter the workforce as apprentices, interns or for paid work include thorough curricula on discrimination and handling racism at the workplace.
- Employ experts from within Singapore to get this path on equality for all, without discrimination and racism, as this has to be the State's agenda on equality, diversity and inclusivity.

It is crucial now that globalised and highly digitised Singapore makes drastic changes to recalibrate its value code on unabridged compliance to equality for the people, for the world and for peace, so as to return, as it were, to the old days of Temasek, when people here depended on each other, and were more ready to form bonds of friendship and respect.

Braema Mathiaparanam (Mathi) is a third-generation Malayan and second-generation Singaporean. She is a Ceylonese Tamil who grew up speaking English, Malay and Tamil, with literacy in English and Malay. Currently an independent researcher and writer, she has worked as a teacher, journalist and researcher, and in organisational development and corporate communications. She focuses on research, advocacy, strategic visioning and training on issues such as gender, migrant workers, social protection, human rights, and business and human rights. She has led and founded some non-governmental organisations in Singapore and for the region. She was also a two-term Nominated Member of Parliament. She has published book chapters, articles, and reports to, and for, organisations including the United Nations and think-tanks in Southeast Asia.

5

Can Harmony Inhibit Cohesion?

VISWA SADASIVAN

"Why are Indians so smelly?... Why are you so dark?... How can you eat such dirty food?" These were the words of endearment from my close Chinese friends when I was growing up in Kampong Bahru in the 1960s. Sometimes, we would end up in a fist fight in the back alley. Other times, I would respond in equal measure. Yet, they were always my buddies.

I also remember an incident when an ethnic Indian friend yelled back with fury at a Chinese friend for calling him *maama*. I asked him why he was so upset about being called *maama* when it simply means "uncle" in Tamil. He didn't know why. It appeared that he felt "obliged" to feel offended.

These negative encounters often presented positive outcomes. We learnt much about each other's cultures, customs, superstitions and languages. We understood each other and became closer. We acknowledged our differences, and learnt to accept, and even appreciate, them. What helped very much was that we often hung out in each other's homes. In fact, we were involved in each other's

Can Harmony Inhibit Cohesion?

culture. We knew each other well enough to give the benefit of the doubt. It wasn't a smooth journey. The road was often rough, with sharp bends with hardly any signage. The fun was in journeying together in trust. This is what made us a community.

The hard truth is that we often become closer after pulling through a rough patch.

In the same vein, my wife and I agree that we shouldn't be too concerned about having arguments. The fights allow us to understand each other better, especially what our dislikes are. This is a continuous process as we all change, over time, many times. On the contrary, several couples I know who avoided arguments or unpleasant situations altogether faced serious problems later in their marriage.

It is possible for us to live under the same roof and be strangers. There's minimal or perfunctory interaction, and an unwillingness to expose our vulnerabilities. We abet a situation where there's harmony, but little or no cohesiveness. It's like skating on a frozen lake – it's smooth and you don't know where it's thin ice. All it takes is a crack for you to go under, in shock, feeling betrayed.

Rehabilitating negative sentiments

Some argue that we need racial harmony before we can become a cohesive society. For me, it's important to strive for these to be mutually reinforcing. Racial harmony is a necessary condition for law and order, socio-political and economic progress, peace, and peace of mind. But an excessive emphasis on harmony is likely to result in a false sense of cohesiveness, which, in turn, could result in complacency. Just because you don't say it, or aren't "allowed" to say it, it doesn't mean that you don't feel negative sentiments.

In such a scenario, deep sentiments of prejudice can't find an outlet. They don't get challenged. Worse, because we tend to hang out with like-minded people, there's an echo chamber effect that affirms these sentiments. Prejudice becomes entrenched. It's subterranean and insidious.

Another consequence of a relentless, unmitigated pursuit of racial harmony is that we systematically lose the faculty for sensing, or discussing, racial discord. We avoid talking about racism or prejudice because it could affect harmony. Through songs and speeches, we keep affirming aspiration as reality. We believe what we want to believe.

> **An excessive emphasis on harmony is likely to result in a false sense of cohesiveness, which could result in complacency. Just because you don't say it, or aren't "allowed" to say it, doesn't mean you don't feel negative sentiments.**

Thus, we lose the ability to sense anomalies – shifts that are taking place around us – because they don't fit into the neat framework of "regardless of race". Those who expose cracks in the system, say, through theatre or commentaries, are viewed as heretics with mischievous intent. We reject them because they desecrate the temple we have built.

Teachers are scared to discuss racial issues with their increasingly curious, and perhaps misled, students. Many of our younger political leaders aren't confident enough to address such issues beyond platitudes and within the safe confines of predictable, scripted lines.

Can Harmony Inhibit Cohesion?

Risk of being overrun by social media sentiments

As a result, we have become a society seriously underprepared for what the Internet and social media have unleashed – the truth about us. This truth looks uglier than it really is. This is because we have been living in a pseudo-utopian state where harmony is the order of the day. It's not sustainable.

It doesn't seem to take much for us to be shocked, disgusted and seek punishment when confronted by what some define as racism. We have witnessed a series of incidents in the past couple of years in particular. Social media empowerment has created new heights in vigilantism. The "call out" and "me too" culture has weaponised hurt and anger. This has emboldened some social media influencers to wilfully amplify mistakes and, perhaps inadvertently, create a culture of distrust predicated on a binary definition of right and wrong.

Much of what we are witnessing is a result of decades of not being able to, and not needing to, deal with racial issues. It is not that they didn't exist. They were pent-up. For the sake of harmony, we played them down, or swept them under the mat. Tolerance became the mantra. For the incorrigible, there was the Internal Security Act and the Sedition Act. Everything was under control. Or so it appeared.

When the "brownface" incident happened in July 2019, it was like all hell broke loose. It was about a TV advertisement in which a well-known ethnic Chinese actor was portrayed as a Chinese, Malay, Indian and Eurasian. To depict an Indian man, he painted his face brown. Yes, perhaps the advertising agency could have been more sensitive. Quite a few of my ethnic Indian friends and I couldn't see why this was treated as a cardinal sin warranting such vitriolic reaction. It hit an ugly note when Internet celebrity Preetipls and her brother Subhas Nair, a musician, put out a rap video clip online with extreme language targeted at the Chinese community. Interestingly, this drew both strong support and criticism, mainly from younger Singaporeans (across ethnicities) and from establishment figures and older Singaporeans, respectively. It was polarising.

In June 2021, there was the incident involving a polytechnic lecturer who was caught on video harassing a mixed-race couple with racist remarks. Unlike the "brownface" incident, this was clearly a case of racism and prejudice. The polytechnic terminated his services. This incident shows that, beneath the veneer of harmony, we are likely to find deep-seated prejudice that never had the chance to be challenged. Rehabilitation is possible only if the issue is allowed to surface.

A month earlier, there was the case of the ethnic Malay couple whose bridal photograph was used by the People's Association (PA) as a standee in a Hari Raya event. The bride accused the PA of using the photograph inappropriately and without consent. The PA apologised. She then alleged that the incident showed racism. While I appreciate her anger, I couldn't get my head around what in this incident made it racist.

We have become a society seriously underprepared for what the Internet and social media have unleashed – the truth about us. This truth looks uglier than it really is, because we have been living in a pseudo-utopian state where harmony is the order of the day. It's not sustainable.

Can Harmony Inhibit Cohesion?

The PA was certainly guilty of being racially insensitive. To be racist, the act needed to be motivated by prejudice, discrimination or antagonism.

Unfortunately, what we are seeing is a bird-out-of-the-cage syndrome. After years of being forced to be restrained, social media has empowered us to speak up and speak out against racism, discrimination and prejudice with backing from like-minded voices, some beyond our borders. I am seeing the dangerous tendency of being overly liberal in defining and calling out racism. I believe there's a distinct and necessary difference between racialisation and racism.

Agreeing on how to talk openly

What's important and necessary, going forward, is that we establish and agree on clear guidelines for engaging each other on sensitive issues such as race and religion. The default position can no longer be that "it's sensitive", so we don't talk about it. This will only provoke unrestrained conversations online.

The only way for the discourse to become more balanced and honest, without being vitriolic, is for a lot more discussions to take place outside of social media. The discussions should not be propagandistic. They need not get out of control if moderated by credible, experienced individuals. Perhaps the time has come for us to have more open discussions. Surveys show that the vast majority of us eschew racism and bigotry. Let this truth surface. Let's have greater faith in Singaporeans.

For us to be able to strike that balance between racial harmony and cohesion, we should address three key needs.

First, the ethnic minority communities need to feel safe and secure, and know that they have institutionalised recourse. This is where legislation and regulations, such as the proposed Maintenance of Racial Harmony Act, serve an important purpose. I don't see why the Presidential Council for Minority Rights can't play a more proactive role in arbitrating critical developments that affect ethnic minorities. Alternatively, Singapore could create an office of the ombudsman for racial matters.

Second, we should eliminate, or at least reduce, mixed signals that could make the ethnic minority communities feel second-class. In this regard, there needs to be a review of the role and relevance of ethnic self-help organisations and Special Assistance Programme (SAP) schools. Even more importantly, political leaders should avoid essentialism. This legitimises racial stereotypes. More insidiously, it promotes the unsubstantiated view that when it comes to accepting a Prime Minister, the Chinese majority would choose ethnic affinity over merit.

Third, the minorities should feel there are enough neutral arbiters who have a loud-enough voice to speak up for them. These would be accomplished individuals who are known for their social and political autonomy. When they speak up, they will be heard. They can help prevent situations from getting out of control by mediating behind the scenes. The government should welcome and encourage this development. It should most certainly avoid inducting these individuals.

The time is now for honest conversation
I believe the government under the late founding Prime Minister Lee Kuan Yew did absolutely the right thing in banning open discussion on race and religion. This was announced right after

Can Harmony Inhibit Cohesion?

Singapore's worst racial riots on 21 July and 2 September 1964. The 1960s, '70s and '80s were a period of adjustment for the people of Singapore – securing a job, educating our children, and learning to trust across racial boundaries, yet again. The focus had to be on racial and religious harmony based on the principle of equal opportunities.

Hence, institutionalised means were created to ensure a healthy mingling of the races. This included mainstream schooling for all, while shutting down the Chinese-medium schools in the early 1970s. The introduction of national service in 1967 forced 18-year-old Singaporean men to soldier together, regardless of race. In 1989, the Ethnic Integration Policy was introduced to break up and prevent HDB ethnic enclaves.

In September 1965, then-PM Lee spoke with conviction that "over 100 years ago, this was a mudflat… ten years from now, this will be a metropolis". There was no way he would have been able to achieve this – provide jobs and give dignity to the people – if there had been no racial and religious harmony.

As a member of an ethnic minority community, I am grateful to the pioneering leaders for laying a solid foundation for us to live in harmony. Even though the Chinese constitute the vast majority, we have committed to be a Singaporean Singapore, regardless of race. Yet, in the complex world we live in today, there's a real risk that we could lose what we have built. Given the plethora of voices and the increasing menace of fake news, it cannot be business as usual.

To remain harmonious for the long haul, we must be prepared for the disruption, and perhaps even despair, that comes with having more robust and honest conversations. I am confident that we will emerge stronger. Let's have faith in the strength that comes from five decades of living together in harmony.

Viswa Sadasivan is a socio-political commentator, speaker and facilitator. He has interviewed global leaders including the late Mr Lee Kuan Yew and President Barack Obama, and moderated over 300 policy forums in Singapore and globally. As founder-CEO of Strategic Moves – a corporate strategy consultancy – he has trained more than 10,000 public and private sector leaders. He served on several national committees and public sector boards. As a national serviceman, he rose to the rank of Colonel and was Deputy Director Joint Operations, Singapore Armed Forces. In 2015 he launched the online interview-discussion programme *Inconvenient Questions* (IQ). In 2021 he launched IQ International, a monthly forum for honest, insightful conversations on pressing issues. He has a master's in public administration from Harvard University's Kennedy School of Government, and served as a Nominated Member of Parliament.

6
Look Beyond Colour

KANNAN CHANDRAN

I was fortunate to be born colour-blind.

Not literally. But in my view of humanity. I don't see races. Or other differentiators like religion or gender. I see the person. I see ability, talent, spirit. I feel chemistry, camaraderie, companionship.

As a journalist and media practitioner since the 1980s, I've met a wide variety of people; from heads of state to celebrities; brand builders to youngsters who will one day rise to prominence. Hence, I have contacts and friends from a range of countries in various industries.

Forging bonds with people is not difficult to do. An open mind and a willingness to find common ground will aid this process. It's more difficult if you impose conditions upon yourself that limit who you can interact with, in areas such as religion, gender, culture and race. But when faced with someone who has such impositions placed upon them, I try as much as possible to be accommodating, within reason and without compromising my own principles and life choices.

Unless you've chosen the life of a hermit, connecting with people is an integral aspect of one's life journey. There will be lots of lessons to be learnt and experiences to be shared. Besides the human interaction, it provides perspective to widen my worldview, offering insights into how others live their lives, and what is important to them. Chemistry is helpful in adding fizz and sparkle to that connection, resulting in memorable moments.

At a professional level, as I delve deeper, past the borders of the other person's life and expectations, I try and develop a strategy that will allow for mutually beneficial collaboration, at a level that is comfortable to all parties.

The curiosity to learn about other people and cultures has enriched my life. It's taught me how we are wonderfully different in some respects, but, as well, the similarities we share. It offers insights into how other communities live and what they are going through to keep the social cohesion strong. How their cultures have evolved over time, resulting in magnificent traditions that are several times older than what we have in Singapore.

Arriving on many boats, for a new life together

For a nation that gained independence in 1965, Singapore has changed dramatically in the years since; physically, for sure, as evidenced in the sparkling skyline, but as well emotionally, as a nation striving to cope with the constant push to be a lead actor on the regional stage with aspirations to make it to the global platform.

To achieve all that it has, the citizens had to come together, work together and live together.

Not an easy feat, given the different directions the immigrant boats sailed in from, carrying people of various races and ethnicities, customs, traditions, thinking and expectations. And they got off the boats to take on a range of different vocations that would – each, in its own big or small way – help to build the country.

While their backgrounds may have been different, the common element of being a foreigner trying to make a new home in a strange land among such a variety of people was a common thread of opportunity and adventure for the new settlers trying to carve their place on this sunny tropical island.

My parents were on such a boat, arriving from Kerala, South India, in the early 1950s. From a large, coastal land mass and a settled way of life, they found themselves on a small island heaving with change. They could fall back on the company of Malayali families from Kerala, but since they were fluent in English, they found it easy also to interact with members of other communities and cultures in their new home.

I was born in Singapore, and I had no say in the matter. I had no say in anything at the start, such as where I was to be born and when I would open my eyes to life on this planet. I also had no say about the race I would be born as.

As these key aspects of my arrival on the planet were well and truly out of my hands, I have accepted them as a given. I can't change these things.

I've been fortunate to live in a country that has seen relative peace for many decades since its independence. It's allowed me to progress at my own pace, without forcing restrictions or requirements upon me, other than National Service, when boys in their late teens disrupt their studies to serve the country.

My parents were open-minded about their expectations when they sailed out to Singapore. They wanted a new start and while there were friends and some relatives from India here, they were not the sort to cling to the old ways to preserve heritage and culture. They appreciated what their country of birth offered, but they were also curious to discover how they could contribute to this new melting pot of people they were now a part of.

Our neighbours hailed from various races and communities, held different beliefs, and we interacted with all of them. We appreciated what their cultures had to offer, from the music to the literature and, of course, the delicious food, the quickest way to connect!

My upbringing was centred on activities involving the library, sports fields and the arts. That opened up connections with an even wider array of friends and interests.

We would play football, a rag-tag group of boys in the neighbourhood with varying skills, on a perilous slope, a raucous bunch who would keep chasing for goal till the sun set and you could barely make out the ball. We seem nowadays to have lost that opportunity to have regular pick-up games. Now, everything follows a more formal process and it's about who has the cash to book a court or a field, which makes it difficult for everyone, regardless of standing and means, to join in.

While my parents' generation of pioneering nation-builders were still finding their way around a mixed community, they managed to build a foundation upon which their children could continue that process. Public housing, infrastructure projects and long-term plans were underway, and their toil and sacrifice paved the way for future generations. The beginnings of multiracial living were already evident then; a result of a greater need.

My parents didn't try and ram culture or religion down my throat. I was allowed to explore my interests and indulge many of my curiosities. I was enrolled in a Catholic school for the education it offered, not because that was my religious belief. My classmates in St Joseph's Institution turned out to be a mixed bunch from many walks of life and holding different religious beliefs and worldviews. Many have settled overseas in an array of industries, but we are still in contact thanks to technology, but, more importantly, because of the shared desire to stay connected.

As an Indian, I am in the minority in Singapore. The Chinese community dominates the population ratio, followed by the Malays, then Indians, and then the grouping of races that fall into the vague, catch-all category of "Others".

I've always looked at this as a convenience for the system. The world likes to pigeonhole things. Makes for easier filing and data entry. It's only relevant at home, because once you're out on the road, you tend to shed your racial distinctiveness, opting to be "Singaporean" and flashing that red passport. That sense of identity seems to be lost at home for some reason, where many fall back into racial differentiation, educational institutions, companies or industries.

The "major drama" of interracial marriage

Marrying out of one's race used to be – and probably still is, albeit perhaps to a lesser extent – a major drama, whether it's for religious, status or racial reasons. Once you put people together, you're going to find new partnerships forming.

Marrying out of my race was never an issue for me, and posed no problems because neither one of us bothered about race; and as long as we both didn't have to compromise unduly, it was just fine. Finding the right person was more important. Not being influenced by other parties probably helped reduce unnecessary churning and annoyance.

Sometimes, knowing your own mind and having a thick-enough skin helps to get past prejudices and unwarranted expectations. Back in the day, the difference – my wife is Chinese – would draw a lot of looks, but we would just ignore it. Over time, inter-marriages have become more common and more readily accepted.

My generation grew up mixing easily and finding the positives in most things that were shaping a young nation. There was a sense of wonder at skyscrapers and malls, and the ongoing physical changes taking place.

The next generation had access to a much easier life, but many were struggling with an education system that was more about performance and good grades, to be relevant to the needs of a rapidly changing world. They were thrown into a cauldron of high-intensity tuition and self-enrichment classes. Forced by parents to achieve top grades and qualify for good schools, they were probably robbed of opportunities to grow up, and interact, with other children. Their best friend was probably the computer.

> **The younger generation had access to a much easier life, but were thrown into a cauldron of high-intensity tuition... they were probably robbed of opportunities to grow up, and interact, with other children.**

Look Beyond Colour

I was surprised when one of the interns at my office commented that she was enjoying her first *roti prata* ever, during a welcome lunch. Her diet had consisted predominantly of Chinese food and pasta dishes.

I asked her why she hadn't tried any of the other cuisines in a food paradise like Singapore. She explained that her close friends were all Chinese. She did say she had fellow students of other races in her cohort, but she didn't know them well. She said she wanted to get good grades and a good job, so that would be her focus.

Faultlines exist in every society. While managing homogeneous societies may be viewed as less complex with fewer variables in the equation, human nature seems to be such that there will always be ways to find sub-divisions and points of differentiation. Besides, hierarchies inevitably form within society to create the required tension to preserve political dominance.

In some countries, a dominant race will assert itself – apartheid in South Africa or the *bumiputera* policy in Malaysia are examples. If you withhold knowledge and reduce opportunities for one or more groups of people, you'll only have a disenfranchised and stratified society that will fight against the system rather than fight alongside it.

In a multiracial society, you have the different races and religions that add their unique spices to the mix. Singapore has opted for the course of equality amongst the races as its driving force towards onward progress. It's stated in the National Pledge – "one united people, regardless of race, language or religion, to build a democratic society, based on justice and equality". Words to live by, and generally an aspiration that has been realised to some extent.

KANNAN CHANDRAN

Welcoming the new waves of immigrants

With people being Singapore's only natural resource, there weren't too many options but to have a potent, effective and efficient workforce.

It was a plan that worked, drawing multinational companies to the island and accelerating the economy to several decades of continued success. The effort involved pulling together with a common vision.

But even in a small, seemingly smoothly ticking society, the occasional issues will surface. As a declining fertility rate sets the government wondering who will make up the workforce of the future, what can't be fulfilled locally will have to be imported. It's a practical economic argument. But how to achieve this without upsetting the racial balance?

The arrival of foreigners to take on the menial jobs that Singaporeans are reluctant to do was less of a concern than those who came in to fill roles in information technology, human resources, and in leadership positions in large corporations. Singapore benefited in the past from standing on the shoulders of foreign giants, and it was acceptable because we had a lot to learn. But to stand shoulder-to-shoulder with a foreigner and yet be passed over for these positions rankles.

If we consider that the bulk of Singapore's population hails from migrant stock, who worked together with the welcoming

> **We ought to spend equal, if not more, time talking about the similarities that we should continue to develop as Singaporeans. I believe that would be more meaningful and useful.**

local Malay communities to build a country, why should we get upset with this continuing trend?

While those who are here for a few generations will call this home, there will be new waves of migrants who will fly in and try to establish roots.

It's a necessary part of Singapore's DNA to have this thinking. Just as my parents assimilated rather than trying to fit into a displaced old-world community, newcomers to Singapore today should mix with local communities rather than just seeking out their own kind.

Similarly, as Singaporeans themselves become more global, the opportunities to shine in other lands will emerge, and we will be the strangers in a strange land vying for jobs over there.

Through the years, the occasional issue of race pops up as something that the government feels it needs to address at a national level. These are reminders of what could get out of control, if not for the rules and laws in place. But, maybe our relationships with other Singaporeans aren't as fragile or tenuous as they are made out to be. The actions of a few seldom reflect the thinking of the masses. But the concept of the noisy minority seems to have entrenched itself in this era of social media and unverified online commentary, to a point that any small utterance or faux pas is viewed as a potential spark that could lead to a wildfire.

Ultimately, these serve as constant reminders of the differences that still exist in our society. Perhaps we ought to spend equal, if not more, time talking about the similarities that we should continue to develop as Singaporeans. I believe that would be more meaningful and useful.

KANNAN CHANDRAN

Kannan Chandran is the founder of E-Quill Media, which publishes books, magazines and websites, including the award-winning current affairs and lifestyle site www.storm-asia.com. He has experienced the changing phases of the media industry, starting off with newspapers before moving to print magazines and books, and now enjoys the virtual and mobile age.

Racial Integration: Lessons from a Lifetime

KIRPAL SINGH

Allow me to begin with a confession: I am passionate, very passionate, about this topic. Why? Because for my entire life so far – I am now near 73 – I have experienced plenty of racism (yes, here in my beloved Singapore) and I yearn for the day that no one – not a Malay or an Indian or a Chinese or a Eurasian or a Caucasian – anyone – will ever be judged and responded to according to his or her ethnic, racial or religious affiliation. This is, clearly, a huge challenge to my fellow Singaporeans.

Racial prejudice runs deep

For prejudice, it seems, is more than skin-deep: it is very, *very* deep. It goes right to our heart and our bones, and all too frequently it begins with our skin. Yes, skin-colour is often where this deep-seated bias begins. There is no rational explanation why this ought to be so. Study after study shows the prevalence of racism, overt and covert. Yes, the stats rise and fall but, beneath it all, prejudice and bias prevail without fail.

I want to share a personal example. Many years ago, my niece, who had studied law at Queen Mary College, London, applied for an executive position with a Singapore bank. Over the phone, the bank manager asked if she could speak, read and write Chinese. She said yes, emphatically. They then spoke in Mandarin. The conversation lasted for quite a while, with both sides confirming that my niece's application was successful and that she would begin work in about a week.

> **I wear a turban – and this, it seems, is where the problem truly lies... this is all so very ironic, and reminds us just how profound the impact of colonisation can be.**

Well, guess what? On the third day after this telephone chat, the manager called and ruefully said, sorry, she did not get the job. When my niece persisted and asked why, the manager replied that they needed her to personally meet and greet the bank's clients and even though she spoke excellent Chinese, because she was not Chinese – and was, he added for good measure, visibly of dark complexion – the clients (mostly Chinese) would not be pleased.

This in the proud Lion City proclaiming to the world how so wonderfully multiracial harmony existed and formed the basis of all human engagements and activity.

The above can be totally understood by someone like the present writer who, for his entire life (save these last four to five years) has been colourfully plagued by fist-fights and verbal abuse arising out of catcalls and racial slurs! From age six (when I was brought here to Singapore from the little village of Batu Gajah in Perak, Malaysia) to even now (though these days the catcalls have almost disappeared, and the underlying racism is signalled in other, sometimes subtle, ways), I have continued to be the subject of what I can honestly term abuse!

I wear a turban – and this, it seems, is where the problem truly lies. In other words, if I just donned a cap or a hat or didn't have anything on my head other than hair (or baldness), things would be okay. This is all so very, very ironic, and reminds us just how profound the impact of colonisation can be. So much of what we do and say – indeed of what and who we are – is colonial. I am sure many will take issue with me over this assertion, but I stand by it: we are still under the fetters of our colonial masters.

The role of English in racial integration

We know that English has become willy-nilly the lingua franca of our nation. Our National Language is Malay, but is it not funny that Singaporeans don't speak, read and or write their National Language?

Of course, I am exaggerating for effect, but, in essence, I think I am right. Most Chinese Singaporeans, Indian Singaporeans, Eurasian Singaporeans and *ang moh* Singaporeans (Caucasians who live here) don't actually know Malay very well (of course some do!), and many can't be bothered to master, or even learn, it.

While language may not be the only index of integration across racial boundaries, it can serve to bring peoples of diverse races together. When we can speak the same language, we tend to become closer and friendlier. When and where citizens of a nation don't have a common language they can all converse in, there exist real barriers to effective and affective communication.

Many years ago – more than half a century ago, actually

— our very own poet Lee Tzu Pheng wrote in her memorable poem entitled "My Country and My People":

> My country and my people
> Are neither here nor there —
> Nor in the comfort of my preferences
> If I could even choose.

Looking back at all these years, I realise just what has happened. The Government seems to have decided that, in addition to various official promotions of racial integration, factors such as language would be passively encouraged rather than actively promulgated. I assume this is in confidence. And also in the reckoning that sooner or later the de facto lingua franca of our nation will make itself present. As it has.

One certain way in which a language becomes the language of a nation is through education. Decades ago, the Government decided that, in fairness to all, English should become the main language of our education. And so it has. Our founding father and first Prime Minister was serious when he stated that it would only be English that would serve two important purposes at once: become the nation's voice to the external world, as well as a voice for its own citizens.

However, it must be clearly stated, also, that important government messages and announcements and broadcasts are made in all four of our official languages: Malay, English, Chinese and Tamil.

It is early days yet to conclude to what extent racial integration is realised — or can be realised — through the use of a common language. I suspect that the answer to this troubling and troublesome question is: to a large extent. But in a very cosmopolitan society, this response must be handled with care in order not to stoke latent emotions which may be riled by a sense of loss or gain. Mr Lee Kuan Yew was very clear when he pronounced that English would be the language of education and hence of administration in Singapore. He had his detractors but not many really argued too strongly about the final decision.

For what it is worth, I can personally attest to the fact that English has more than served us well. We Asians tend to be generally conservative, clinging strongly to our own traditions and customs and ways of behaving.

> **As a pragmatic people, we can adjust anything and everything should the need for such adjustments arise.**

This is reflected in several different but obvious ways: the ways we dress when celebrating our own festivals, the details we pay attention to when celebrating occasions near and dear to us, and the general ways in which we conduct our daily routines.

If little Singapore (our big Indonesian neighbour once called us "a little red dot") has demonstrated one thing to the world, it is this: that, as a pragmatic people, we can adjust anything and everything should the need for such adjustments arise.

Thus, to conclude this all-too-brief excursion to the land of controversy and ongoing experiments, allow me to restate that racial integration is a subject fraught with plenty of sense and nonsense. Basically, it is common sense that often prevails in determining priorities and urgencies pertaining to our nation and our fellow citizens.

KIRPAL SINGH

We must integrate – but we also know that we cannot simply integrate by flatly doing this or that. It is – as they say – a work in progress. It may be for the next generation of Singaporeans to conclude whether the path my generation decided upon as best turns out to be so.

Dr Kirpal Singh is a creativity guru, the first non-American to be admitted to the American Creativity Association, where he was elected Vice-President in charge of international outreach. He was the first Singaporean to be awarded a Colombo Plan scholarship to pursue a PhD in English at the University of Adelaide. For 45 years, he taught at the National University of Singapore and Nanyang Technological University, and was among the pioneering faculty of Singapore Management University, appointed to launch a creativity studies programme which was mandatory for all students. He left university life in 2017 to join Training Vision Institute as Director, where he established a Centre for Educational Leadership. He is a writer of poems, stories and critical articles, with more than 20 books to his name. He also conducts training in creativity and offers advice as a futurist for major corporations including IBM, L'Oréal and 3M.

8

CMIO:
An Anglo-Chinese Perspective

MARGARET THOMAS

Mine might be the only Singapore identity card that declares the owner's race to be "Anglo-Chinese". I've not seen any other ICs that say this. But then, we don't really go around looking at other people's ICs, do we?

There's a bit of a story to my IC. Until the 1990s, our identity cards were laminated bits of paper. On the back, the information about the owner included not just "Race" but also "Dialect group". Mine said "English" for both fields. This irked me because it was a half-truth. Yes, my father was English, but my mother was Peranakan Chinese, and I felt that if there really was a need for an official declaration of my "race", it should be accurate.

In 1988, I decided to see if I could do anything about this half-truth, and queried the National Registration Department. A spokeswoman explained that while there was nothing in the statutes that said a child should take the father's race, the law did say a child should take the father's surname, unless the father was not known. So the practice was, when dealing with the children of mixed marriages, to assign the father's race to the child.

But the department, she said, did want to be as accurate as possible about a person's race, so if I wanted to, I could apply to change my race classification. However, she explained, before allowing such changes, they would have to be convinced that the child of a mixed marriage had indeed been exposed to the culture and customs of both races. So, if I wanted to change my race to, say, Anglo-Chinese, I would have to show some proof of my Chineseness.

This irked me even more. (Bureaucracy often irks me.) Wasn't it good enough that my parents' races were clearly stated on my birth certificate, and that I had grown up in Singapore and gone to local schools? The spokeswoman seemed to agree, and said it should be easy enough for me to get the change made.

"No 'race' on ICs, please, we're Singaporeans"

I didn't follow up on this at that point. I just grumbled about the matter in a column titled "No 'race', please, we're Singaporeans". This was in the November 1988 issue of the now-defunct magazine *Singapore Business*.

I ended the column declaring: "... race, for someone such as me, the product of a mixed marriage, has limited meaning. It is 'nationality' that gives me my identity, for it is the 'Singaporean' tag that tells the world who I am and what I am like. Indeed, this is the case for most Singaporeans, whatever their race and however much pride they may take in being 'Chinese', 'Malay', 'Indian' or 'Other'. This is what nation-building in Singapore has been all about – making sure we are 'one united people regardless of race,

CMIO: An Anglo-Chinese Perspective

language or religion'. We have built such a nation. Is it not time to disregard 'race' on identity cards and other official forms and documents?"

Clearly, in 1988, the time had not come. And today, more than three decades later, clearly it is still not time because we continue to be pigeonholed in our CMIO (Chinese-Malay-Indian-Others) boxes, making our monthly contributions to the race-based SHG (self-help group) funds, struggling in school with mother tongue languages that neither mother nor father may speak, and navigating the EIP (Ethnic Integration Policy) considerations when buying or selling HDB flats.

Before I update my grumble about our racial pigeonholing, I should complete the story about my IC. In 1991 the government announced that the laminated ICs would be replaced with tamper-proof, credit card-sized ones made of durable polycarbonate. The exercise would take several years, it said.

When my turn came in 1992, I once again contacted the National Registration Department. The officer I spoke to on the phone was patient and helpful.

"Why must we have 'race' on our ICs?" I asked him. I don't remember his reply, but we both knew it was a rhetorical question. "If we must have race, then I would like an accurate account of my mixed heritage," I told him.

> Race, for someone such as me, the product of a mixed marriage, has limited meaning. It is "nationality" that gives me my identity, for it is the "Singaporean" tag that tells the world who I am and what I am like.

He said I could apply to have my race changed to "Eurasian".

I said while that would technically be correct, I didn't feel "Eurasian" in the way this was understood and experienced in Singapore and Malaysia, where there is a distinct Eurasian culture and cuisine. I grew up in a Peranakan household eating *ayam buah keluak* and *babi pongteh*; I had no affinity with Eurasian dishes such as *feng* and Devil's curry.

"So what do you want as your race?" he asked.

"How about 'Anglo-Chinese'?" I said.

I heard him open a drawer or a folder, presumably to check a list of acceptable racial classifications, and then he said: "Okay."

And that's how I got a hyphenated-race on my IC in 1992 – long before it was announced, in 2010, that mixed-race couples would from January 2011 be able to opt for double-barrelled race descriptions for their children.

Making that announcement, the Immigration and Checkpoints Authority (ICA) said: "This added flexibility of registering a double-barrelled race is in line with the Government's continual review of its policies in recognition of evolving societal changes. In this instance, we recognise that with the increasing number of inter-ethnic marriages in Singapore, the diversity of Singapore's racial demographics has accordingly also increased."

Time to stop racial pigeonholing?
It's a diversity that will keep increasing. About a fifth of marriages these days are inter-ethnic. With each such marriage, the lines that define the "races" get more and more blurred. It will get to a point where the mix of races is such that "race" becomes meaningless. What then of our CMIO policies? Already there are many who do not easily and happily fit into these constricting racial

pigeonholes. For how much longer can we justify and sustain the CMIO categorisations?

The racial classifications began in the colonial days. When Singapore gained independence, we carried on with these classifications because this was seen, and continues to be seen, as the best way to maintain the multiracial character of our society and to ensure racial harmony. Our immigration policies are calibrated to ensure that, given the varying fertility rates of the various ethnic groups, we maintain the C component of the population at around 76%, with M around 15%, I around 7%, and O around 1%.

But this carefully managed racial harmony has been tested of late. A string of racist incidents went viral in 2021, such as the polytechnic lecturer's haranguing of an interracial couple. As I write this, a rapper of Indian descent has been charged in court with attempting to promote feelings of ill-will between different races and religions.

By sticking these CMIO labels on ourselves, are we making it easier or harder for people to accept someone of a different race, to understand each other better, and to get on better?

The Government now plans to pull together the various laws dealing with racial issues under a new Maintenance of Racial Harmony Act. New measures and sanctions are likely, Home Affairs Minister K. Shanmugam has said. But he added that what is needed beyond the laws and sanctions is an effort to "try and shape behaviour, including social behaviour and social norms". "The focus," he said, "must really be to try and get people to understand each other better, and get on better."

Presumably, when this new Act is introduced, there will be discussion and debate in Parliament and also in the public arena. We should look at the state's race-based policies – the CMIO classification, the mother tongue second language policy, the SHGs, the EIP – and we should talk frankly about how much they have helped or hindered racial harmony.

In 2017, Prime Minister Lee Hsien Loong spoke about this: "Sometimes we think we have arrived, and we can do away with [multiracial] provisions and rules which feel like such a burden. But in fact, it is the other way around. It is precisely because we have these provisions and rules, that we have achieved racial and religious harmony. We have not yet arrived at an ideal state of accepting people of a different race."

Let's talk about that ideal state and what we can do to make it happen. Let's talk about how the CMIO categories are increasingly out of sync with evolving societal changes such as the growing number of interracial marriages and partnerships. By sticking these CMIO labels on ourselves, are we making it easier or harder for people to accept someone of a different race, to understand each other better, and to get on better? Is keeping strictly to that 76%-15%-7%-1% racial segmentation really the best way for us to maintain the multiracial character of our society?

I think it really is time to move beyond the CMIO racial pigeonholes, the labels that are making us overly conscious of our race, the policies that may be deepening rather than diminishing the divisions between the races. It is time to let our multiracial society develop more naturally.

Perhaps I am being naive in saying this. But it is the naivete of those for whom "multiracial" describes not just the society in which we live, but our lived reality. We are born of two or more races, exposed to two or more cultures. This makes us rather less inclined to the tribalism that can lead to close-mindedness, bigotry, and racism. It makes us more inclined to see people simply as people, regardless of their race, language, or religion.

Margaret Thomas was a journalist for more than 25 years at *The Business Times*, *The Singapore Monitor*, *AsiaOne*, and *TODAY*. She now works primarily on book projects and, in various voluntary roles, on the pursuit of gender equality and an open, informed, and inclusive society. She was a founder member of AWARE (Association of Women for Action & Research) in 1984/85 and is its current President. She has also been involved in civil society organisations and initiatives such as TWC2, the Singapore Women's Hall of Fame, and the Singapore Advocacy Awards.

"One United People": A View from the Singapore Eurasian Community

ALEXIUS A. PEREIRA

When asked to share my thoughts about the phrase "one united people", it occurred to me that the term might not refer only to Singapore, but also to my own community: the Eurasians of Singapore. And the more I thought about it, I realised that many of the issues are the same for both the nation and my community. In other words, I asked myself: "Are we – Singaporeans – one united people?", and similarly: "Are we – the Eurasians – one united people?"

How other societies have coped with multiculturalism
The context of the phrase "one united people" comes from Singapore's national pledge, which reads: "We, the citizens of Singapore, pledge ourselves as one united people, regardless of race, language or religion..."

A View from the Singapore Eurasian Community

Implicit in the phrase written by former Cabinet Minister S. Rajaratnam is the acknowledgement that race, language and religion could derail unity. This is because Singapore, like many modern societies, is racially, linguistically and religiously heterogeneous, made up of peoples of different backgrounds. In such "multicultural" societies, these racial, linguistic and religious differences may lead to misunderstanding, mistrust and conflict.

Societies have come up with different solutions for the potential problems brought by multiculturalism. Some have tried assimilation, where social and cultural policies are designed to encourage peoples whose culture, language and religion are dissimilar to blend in and become more like the majority. We see such assimilative policies in France, Germany, Thailand and Japan, at various points in their histories.

Some societies have tried to deal with heterogeneity by separating peoples of different races, languages or religions. The most evident was the South African apartheid era, when, as a strategy to dominate the African population, the Caucasian "Whites" ensured that there were dual streams for most aspects of life, including in education, the economy, and even politics. Somewhat similar was the system of segregation in the 1950s in southern USA, where – infamously – "black" people (of African descent) had to sit at the back of buses and restaurants, among other laws.

Some states try amalgamation, in which all the present cultures blend together to try to form a new identity. This "melting pot" concept was used to describe Brazil and the USA, at some points in their respective histories.

Some try multiculturalism as the social and cultural policy itself, which is the acceptance of the country being made up of different peoples with different cultures. This would include countries such as Switzerland, which is made up four different cultures (German, French, Italian and Romansch), and consequently has four national languages. Contemporary Canada espouses a multiculturalism whereby both English and French are recognised as their versions of the national language, and where federal funds are made available to preserve both the Anglophone and Francophone cultures (e.g., for television stations and newspapers).

As implied, multicultural states have experienced varying degrees of "success" at different points in their histories. There have been periods of peace and harmony, but, at other times, tension and strife. Two sad examples have been Bosnia and Rwanda, where racial (tribal), linguistic and religious differences led to internal violence. It is difficult enough to manage any state, but it – probably – is even more difficult to manage a multicultural society.

However, social science research – through studying the more successful multicultural societies – has found that there are some common factors and conditions that can lead to relatively sustained periods of social peace and harmony. The three most prominent conditions are the following:

- When there is power-sharing – where one group does not dominate power and write the rules to benefit itself; that is, all groups in society are politically equal.
- When there is equitable economic distribution – where one group does not appear to have greater economic privileges than the others.

- When there is equal recognition – where every group's culture, traditions, languages and religions are treated with respect.

That being said, the presence of political, economic and socio-cultural equality probably only removes the likelihood of inter-group conflicts (like hatred and violence). There needs to be yet another level up, which is to get the diverse groups in society to feel an attachment and belonging, not just to the country, but also to each other.

The experience of multiracial Singapore

Singapore is a multicultural society that was artificially constructed by the British colonial administration from 1819 onwards. As the British empire expanded, its worldview was shaped to see "peoples" or "races" as economic resources. In Singapore, similar to other British colonies, the British brought in specific races of people to serve in designated sectors of the economy.

For example, the Chinese from the southern provinces were brought in to work as coolies at the ports. Indians from south India were brought in to work in the plantations, and later in the shipyards. Malays from around the region were brought in to work in "the uniformed services", including as policemen.

Within these broad categories, the British even had niche professions, such as bringing in Sikhs to be security guards. The British, thanks to their experience in Hong Kong, brought in the Hainanese to be their chefs, and also encouraged the Shanghainese to be the artistic entrepreneurs in Singapore.

Over a hundred years later, due to the outcomes of the

Second World War, for many of these migrants to Singapore and their descendants, returning to the motherland was not an option. Hence, the government of newly independent Singapore inherited in 1965 a multiracial country, one that had, in the 10 years preceding independence, seen inter-community strife.

The Lee Kuan Yew-led government made the conscious choice to make the communities here share power. Although the Chinese population made up more than three-quarters of the population, the Chinese community agreed not to push for a "Chinese Singapore", in which the main language could have been Mandarin.

The government made meritocracy a foundation for society, whereby opportunities for progression were not restricted to one group, but possible for anyone who worked hard. In other words, the economic system was made fair to all groups.

Lastly, and probably most importantly, the government overtly recognised the minority groups, as laid out in Article 152 of the Singapore Constitution:

1. It shall be the responsibility of the Government constantly to care for the interests of the racial and religious minorities in Singapore.

2. The Government shall exercise its functions in such manner as to recognise the special position of the Malays, who are the indigenous people of Singapore, and accordingly it shall be the responsibility of the Government to protect, safeguard, support, foster and promote their political, educational, religious, economic, social and cultural interests and the Malay language.

A View from the Singapore Eurasian Community

In actual life, the recognition goes beyond words on paper; the government ensures that land for building of places of worship for each community is guaranteed, and that the mass media system in Singapore uses the three main languages of the larger communities – Mandarin, Malay and Tamil – as well as English.

Put in simple terms, the government of Singapore, since 1965, sees Chinese people, Malay people, Indian people, and people of other races, as equally Singaporean. In many ways, the racial policy in Singapore is aligned with the best advice from academic knowledge about stable multicultural societies, and the country's track record since 1965 has been that there have not been serious incidents of inter-racial conflict.

It is worth asking if a lack of conflict in Singapore is the same as being "one united people". But first, let me introduce you to the Eurasians of Singapore.

Singapore Eurasians – dealing with hybridity

Singapore's Eurasians, like Singapore itself, were also artificially created by the British colonial government in Southeast Asia. Eurasians are a community of people who have both European (or Caucasian – as the British called it) and Asian parentage. Some Eurasians emigrated to Singapore after 1819. Some came from Malacca, where there was a community who descended from the intermarriages of colonial Portuguese peoples and the local communities, who could be of Chinese, Malay or Indian descent. Others came from Sri Lanka (or Ceylon, as it was known in the 19th century), where there was a Dutch-Ceylonese Eurasian community known as *burghers*, and from India, where there were Anglo-Indian Eurasians. There were also a few who came from other British colonies, including Hong Kong (Anglo-Chinese Eurasians) and Burma (Anglo-Burmese Eurasians).

There were also first-generation Eurasians who were born in Singapore in the colonial era. Some were born to Caucasian and Asian parents, some others were born to Caucasian and Eurasian parents, and also, born to parents of different Eurasian origins (e.g., a Eurasian father from Malacca of Portuguese descent and an Anglo-Chinese Eurasian mother from Hong Kong). Through the community's own oral history as well as some genealogical studies, Singapore's Eurasians are generally a very hybrid people with multiple ancestries.

However, the British colonial administration in Singapore treated Eurasians as "one race," just as it treated all Chinese, Malays and Indians as if they were one type each, disregarding the huge regional, cultural and linguistic diversity of these peoples. As mentioned earlier, racial groups – in colonial times – served specific economic functions within British colonial society. The Eurasians had their niche: they were recruited to fill the lower ranks of the colonial administration, serving as clerks and junior officers in the civil service.

Many Eurasians in colonial Singapore had a comfortable life as their economic niche was fairly well-paying, enough for many to afford good property in the city centre or in the coastal areas of Katong. But everything changed when the Japanese occupied Singapore. Eurasians were seen as conspirators with the British, and treated with deep suspicion. Many Eurasians perished in Singapore, when sent to the Siam "Death" Railway, or when moved to the "Catholic Colony" in Bahau, Negri Sembilan.

And when independence came, the Eurasians were at a

crossroads. Due to the political and economic uncertainties of Singapore at that time, some emigrated to Australia, Canada and the UK. For those who stayed, there was the promise of a "Singaporean Singapore". This phrase was central to Singapore's separation from Malaysia, as the government in Kuala Lumpur was pursuing a Malay Malaysia as opposed to a Malaysian (i.e. race-neutral) Malaysia.

Many of the Eurasians who chose to remain in Singapore looked forward to this idea. Indeed, one of the most prominent Eurasians of the post-Independence Singapore state and former Minister of Law, Edmund W. Barker, himself a Eurasian, said, when then-Prime Minister Lee Kuan Yew spoke to him about running as a Eurasian in the electoral ward of Tanglin: "No. We don't have Eurasians in Singapore now. Only Singaporeans."

As members of a numerically small community, many Eurasians preferred that Singapore be race-neutral and subscribe only to the broader national identity of "Singaporean", rather than being Chinese, Indian, Malay or Eurasian. After all, why be 1% when you can be part of the 100%?

In the 1980s, the government made a shift to be more "ethnically aware", because it was concerned that Singaporeans were becoming too "Westernised", and wanted to inculcate "Asian values" among Singaporeans. This was articulated through promoting the "mother tongue" for each community, and being ethnically proud of one's ancestry through learning about each group's own history. Many people shifted from being just "Singaporean" to "Chinese Singaporean", or "Singaporean Malay", and so on. Some Eurasians were uncomfortable with this, while others saw this as an opportunity to touch base with their own roots.

For example, some Eurasians today are rediscovering Kristang, a creole of old Portuguese and Malay, spoken mainly in Malacca.

Today, from the perspective of the Eurasian community, most would see themselves as a numerical minority rather than a political, economic or social minority. In 2020, there were around 18,000 Eurasian residents in Singapore, making up 0.3% of the total resident population. Most do not, I think, feel like they have lesser rights and privileges than other groups. In fact, despite the community's small numbers, it is treated as one out of four main communities in the eyes of the government. Eurasians, via the Eurasian Association, are regularly represented at national-level committees, boards and conferences. Over and above this, there is even a Minister (who need not be Eurasian) appointed by the Cabinet to represent the Eurasian community. For the government's term between 2020 and 2025, the Minister was Mr S. Iswaran.

Most Eurasians feel that they have equal economic opportunities and do not feel excluded from public life. But some Eurasians do feel unrecognised... the most common experience is to be asked by unaware Singaporeans of other races: "So, how long have you been in Singapore?"

The state's overt recognition of the Eurasian community says to the community that "you belong". I would further argue, albeit without hard evidence or data, that by my sensing, most Eurasians feel that they have equal economic opportunities and do not feel excluded from public life.

Some Eurasians do feel unrecognised; this happens occasionally when people ask Eurasians – especially those who have

Caucasian features – if they are expatriates. The most common experience is to be asked by unaware Singaporeans of other races: "So, how long have you been in Singapore?" upon which the regular answer might well be: "My family has been in this region for 500 years."

Some Singaporeans also seem unaware of how the Eurasian community contributed to nation-building, as there have been Eurasian Ministers and political office-holders, and even the President of Singapore from 1971 to 1981, Benjamin H. Sheares. However, this is an outcome of being numerically small, and so, it is harder for "our story" to be told. Therefore, when the Eurasian Association asked the government for financial support to develop the Eurasian Heritage Gallery, to tell the Singapore Eurasian story, the National Heritage Board was one of the key supporters.

Despite these small "inconveniences", I would unequivocally state that the government has made every effort to make the Eurasian community feel like they organically belong to Singapore. I also would go out on a limb to assert that most Singapore Eurasians also feel that they do indeed belong to Singapore, one that is "regardless of race, language and religion". In other words, if asked, most Eurasians would be happy to be part of Singapore's "one united people".

"New Eurasians" and other challenges

This is, however, not to suggest that unity is a given, or that cohesion is "natural". As mentioned previously, Singapore Eurasians are very hybrid in terms of their ancestry and background. Therefore, even within the Eurasian community, we have had to make the effort to recognise and celebrate our own diversity.

For example, it would have been convenient and easy to just highlight and celebrate the Portuguese-Malaccan ancestry, as this is the most numerically dominant Eurasian sub-group in Singapore, mainly because the majority of Eurasians who came to Singapore were the Portuguese Eurasians from Malacca. For example, the three most high-profile cultural components of Singapore Eurasian culture all originate from Malacca: the dish known as *curry debal* (sometimes Anglicised as Devil's Curry), the Eurasian dance (performed in traditional Portuguese costumes) and the Kristang creole.

Fully aware of this, the Eurasian Association goes out of its way to regularly feature and celebrate the smaller Eurasian sub-groups, such as the Dutch Eurasians (descended from Ceylon or Indonesia), the Anglo-Burmese (from Burma) and the Anglo-Chinese (from Hong Kong), to show them that they are equally appreciated and encouraged to share aspects of their traditions, so that they feel that they belong equally to the community.

At the same time, the Eurasian Association welcomes all "first-generation" or "new" Eurasians, treating them exactly the same as "old" Eurasians (those who might have been Eurasian for several generations). While it is fairly easy to confer equal status – at least within the Association – and to invite them to participate in the Association's activities,

> **If the Singapore Eurasians can come together despite hugely diverse backgrounds, then Singaporeans of various backgrounds can do the same... by embracing their diversity, and not emphasising the superiority of any one sub-group.**

it is understandable that there might be some hesitation on the part of the new Eurasians. Those of them who have, say, Caucasian American or Australian and Asian parents would not have the immediate connection with the "old Eurasians"; they would not share the history of the Second World War in Singapore, and probably feel the Eurasian cuisine is totally alien.

Still, the Eurasian Association continues to reach out to them, in the hope that they will reciprocate and gradually feel that they belong to the Eurasian community.

Today, in 2021, I would argue that there is a vibrant Eurasian community, in which most Eurasians feel that they belong to the community, and to Singapore at the same time. As Prime Minister Lee Hsien Loong, who was the Guest of Honour at the Eurasian Association's 100th Anniversary Festival in 2019, said in his speech: "Today, your community epitomises and embodies Singapore's multi-racial, multi-religious, and multi-cultural society. In you, there is Singapore, and in Singapore, there is you – more than a little bit! And because of this inclusive psyche, Singaporean Eurasians have immersed themselves in nation building."

Contradictions sometimes work? Multiculturalism as national ethos

The Singapore Eurasian community aspires to be diverse *and* united. Can this be achieved for Singapore? In my view, this is eminently possible, because the conditions for unity are already present: by and large, there is political, economic and cultural equality and equity among the racial and religious groups here in Singapore. In addition, there has been a sustained period of social harmony and lack of conflict among the main groups.

If the Singapore Eurasians can come together despite their hugely diverse backgrounds, then it stands to reason that Singaporeans of various racial, linguistic and religious backgrounds can do the same.

The Eurasians did so by embracing their diversity, and not emphasising the superiority of any one particular sub-group; the numerical majority within the Eurasian community – those of Portuguese Malaccan descent – have been accepting of other lineages, including those who are "new Eurasians".

Just as embracing diversity might be part of the ethos of the Eurasian community, for Singapore, this might be similar to embracing multiculturalism as a key component of the nation's ethos; to celebrate that each group is equally respected and recognised.

Singapore is a contradiction. Contradictions are supposed to be harmful, but sometimes contradictions work.

Singapore was not supposed to survive economically. We were not supposed to overcome the racial divides. Other societies have had huge difficulties trying to maintain racial harmony. Some say: "Because we are many people, we cannot be one united people." But Singapore has managed to bring different peoples together; we have allowed them to retain their cultures and beliefs. We have created safe spaces to share. We have focused on commonalities rather than differences. And so, if we are willing, Singaporeans of all races and cultures can also truly embrace the term "Singaporean", and become "one united people" even more, without having to give up any of our other identities.

A View from the Singapore Eurasian Community

Alexius Pereira has been President of the Eurasian Association, Singapore, since 2018. Previously, he was a lecturer at the Department of Sociology, National University of Singapore. His publications include *Eurasians* (2015, Straits Times Press) and *Singapore Eurasians: Memories, Hopes and Dreams* (co-author, 2017, World Scientific). He has been a member of the National Integration Council since 2018, and the Ministry of Education's COMPASS (Community and Parents in Support of Schools) since 2019.

10

"Is He Chinese?"

KENNETH PAUL TAN

The daughter of John Raymond Francisco and Gladys Olga Klass, whose ancestors were Portuguese and Dutch respectively, my late mother Adeline Catherine Francisco belonged to the Eurasian community in Singapore. When she was alive, she would sometimes share memories of how her parents and grandparents had been pillars of the local Roman Catholic Church and how one of the pews at the Portuguese Mission's St Joseph's Church on Victoria Street had the family name on it. On the rare occasion when we talked about our family history and looked at old sepia-toned family photographs, it was quite clear that my great-grandparents and their children lived a privileged lifestyle in Singapore, involving distinctively European tastes and sensibilities, a love of good food, as well as a rather austere Catholic piety and frequent acts of charity.

My father, Philip Tan Swee, met my mother as young teachers at Fowlie School in the 1960s. His father, a Cantonese-speaking Khek musician from China, had come to Melaka, Malaysia, where he married my grandmother, a Cantonese-speaking Teochew.

"Is He Chinese?"

My father was born in Melaka in the early 1940s before the whole family moved to Singapore.

As a young child growing up in this multicultural family, I spoke English, Malay, and a smattering of Cantonese. My Malay was learnt to a surprisingly fluent level of proficiency from a neighbour who came most days of the week to help with the housework and to look after my brother and me while both our parents were at work. When I reached school-going age, my parents chose Malay, rather than Mandarin, as a second language for me. Singapore's bilingual education policy at the time allowed some flexibility for a biracial child like me to choose a language other than that assigned to the father's official racial identity, which would in my case have been Mandarin.

My parents also thought it a good idea to engage a private tutor to improve my mastery of the Malay language, mainly for me to gain appreciation of the culture. My tutor's interest in the representational power of the Malay language was just as infectious as his command of the rules of that language. *Peribahasa* (proverbs) and *pantun* (a poetic form), for instance, opened my eyes and ears to the intricacies of an immensely beautiful language and culture, which I wish today I had put more effort into learning.

My wife, Clara Lim, is Hokkien. Her paternal grandmother was Peranakan. But her family speaks Cantonese. When my mother was still alive, we all dined together very often. The dinner table was a cacophony of languages, which we used playfully to joke with one another. All of us could, of course, speak English. And that was probably the language we were all most fluent in. All of us, except Clara, could speak Malay. My father, Clara, and her mother could speak Mandarin.

Flora, whom we employed as a domestic worker for over two decades, threw Tagalog into the mix. And Fita, whom we currently employ, takes great pleasure in comparing the Malay we speak in Singapore with Bahasa Indonesia. My mother could also speak the Kristang language, a severely endangered Portuguese creole. I knew a few words and phrases that I could trade with her. But all of us knew what "*O Deus, yo ta mureh!*" meant, a phrase we could exclaim in mock-ecstasy whenever we ate strong-flavoured food like oxtail soup or durian. The phrase means "Oh God, I'm dying!" This, along with other things said – and often deliberately mispronounced – in different languages, was part of the interculturally nonsensical conversations that playfully held our family together.

This is, in fact, my intercultural identity.

A minority within a minority within a minority

But in the eyes of the state, and therefore of much of the society I live in, I am Chinese. My Identity Card says so. And I am often required to say so whenever an official form needs to be filled.

But I am visibly a brown-skinned man. Which frequently attracts the question, "Are you Chinese?", whenever I meet another Singaporean for the first time, even in situations when that is among the least relevant aspects of who I am. Or, more discreetly, they might ask someone else about me: "Is he Chinese?" I mostly attribute these questions to harmless curiosity. In a society conditioned to fit things, people, relationships, and experiences into simple and stable categories, I suppose being curious about things, people, relationships, and experiences that don't fit so neatly should not be a surprise. And curiosity is, after all, healthy,

"Is He Chinese?"

and creates the opportunity for learning. I would like to think so anyway.

And yet, something deep inside me wonders whether behind the question "Are you Chinese?" or "Is he Chinese?" is a judgement of some kind. That, despite my achievements and professional standing, everything in that moment reduces to the sense I get of being deficient, not Chinese enough. Where the unspoken follow-up question is: "If he is Chinese, then why can't he read Chinese or speak Mandarin?"

> **Something deep inside me wonders whether behind the question "Are you Chinese?" or "Is he Chinese?" is a judgement of some kind.**

In school, I had instead learnt Malay, the language of a community that has for decades been characterised through a historically distorted narrative of underperformance, a translucent barrier that members of that community must overcome every day just to dispel the stereotype and prove themselves worthy of the nation's smug benignity. Regular iterations of discreditation, condescension, and indignity can mould the collective mindset about racial difference and relative ability, which members of the minority community may themselves internalise in a tragically self-limiting way. What a heavy burden to carry. It tires me just thinking about it.

Or the follow-up question might be: "If he is Chinese, then why doesn't he look Chinese?" Or: "Why is he so tanned?" Or: "Why is he so dark?" And the thought that this question might be motivated by a deep fear or dislike of darkness crosses my mind. A big part of who I am is Eurasian, a minority group that, for the longest time, had been (un[der])represented in the official "multiracialism" orthodoxy as belonging to that last racial category known as "Others". And even within this minority community, the so-called "upper ten percent" – or "white Eurasians" – were historically at the top of a social hierarchy. Colour has always and everywhere been saturated with affective significance, as much as our liberal sensibilities would like to deny it.

But I also wonder whether these questions have their roots in a still fertile myth of racial purity. Were the questioners uncomfortable with the in-your-face racial hybridity of Eurasians, whose heritage includes "Western culture" that may trigger anxieties about Asian values? Or was it a discomfort with the watering down of Chinese-ness through intermarriage? Were they passively critical of mixed parentage as a sign of inauthenticity or disloyalty?

As a child in the 1970s, when we went out as a family, there were occasional looks of curiosity from strangers who I believe meant no harm or disrespect. After all, I grew up seeing my father's Chinese family welcome my Eurasian mother and her family with open arms. And this was just as true of my maternal family's affection for my father and his family. So, I was never really confronted by hostility towards biracial families and people. I only really felt the sting of it through the second-hand experience of reading about that undergraduate who, at a student forum in 2005, had asked a senior politician a question about interracial couples, which he said, "made his skin crawl".

And then, seeing that viral video of a 60-year-old Chinese male lecturer berating an interracial couple on a public street, the man part-Indian and part-Filipino and the woman part-Chinese and part-Thai. I wanted so much to think of these as exceptional cases, when just a handful of people perhaps lost control on a particularly bad day. But I cannot help but wonder if such a view is more widely held, suppressed only by political correctness and state policing.

And so, in Singapore, my intercultural identity is constantly being boxed in situations in which I am reminded of my status as a minority within a minority within a minority.

Glass ceilings everywhere

At one basic level, I know in the broadest terms what it feels like to be in the minority, especially when that minority is viewed by the majority – and sometimes by the minority itself – through hardwired stereotypical lenses, described through language that betrays a bullying culture. I am reminded of that scene in the 1981 movie *Chariots of Fire* when the Jewish Olympic champion sprinter Harold Abrahams explains how he got admitted to Cambridge University: "I'm what I call semi-deprived. It means they lead me to water, but they won't let me drink."

There are glass ceilings everywhere. But their existence and effect are notoriously difficult to know, and much more difficult to prove, without sounding churlish. It is one of the most humiliating things to have to explain how latent discrimination limited one's prospects. Many would rather just say they were not good enough.

All of this has subtly influenced how minoritised people are (mis)recognised, forcing them sometimes against their better judgement to respond in ways that limit their sense of self in order that they may be acceptably legible to people conditioned to think in monocultural and stereotypically hierarchical terms.

Though I can empathise deeply with this, I cannot claim to have been disadvantaged extensively in my own life, which has mainly been a privileged one. I was lucky enough to have parents who worked hard and made good choices. Lucky to have been surrounded by enough people who supported me generously and helped me out when I needed help. And lucky enough to have had opportunities come my way at the right time and place.

> **It is one of the most humiliating things to have to explain how latent discrimination limited one's prospects. Many would rather just say they were not good enough.**

And though I know what it feels like to be "othered" and even excluded when it matters, I am also very aware of my privilege. That my intercultural and intersectional identity has dealt me many cards to play beyond my minoritised status. Put another way, I may hit a glass ceiling in one room, but I have keys to open a door to another.

Other people may not be so lucky. Their intersectional identity, in contrast, traps them in the most disadvantaged positions in society, where their race, gender, sexuality, socio-economic circumstances, political convictions, and other facets of their identity all converge upon, and mutually reinforce, a hyper-minoritised status that leads to ridicule, exclusion, and real material disadvantage. Race, its intersectional relationship with other facets of identity, and its intercultural fluidity can be a resource for some, but it can just as easily be a painful burden for others. And carrying a painful burden that is scarcely visible in the series of sprints that

"Is He Chinese?"

constitute our lives is a terrible disadvantage in a competitive society that is quick to label.

So, when I think of the problem of inequality in Singapore, which has in recent years received greater public attention, I do not necessarily think, in the first instance, about the abstract measurements of income or wealth distribution. Neither do I care very much for assertions that we should tackle poverty and not bother very much about inequality, as if the two were separate issues, one simply a distraction. I am more interested in how people are systematically excluded, especially in insidious ways that limit their prospects, while ideological pieties such as "meritocracy" serve to obfuscate these exclusions by entrenching beliefs about how it is the individual, and not latent social attitudes and institutional inequalities, who must be credited and blamed for their success and failure.

In today's Singapore, we can all be very thankful that we almost never see racial violence and brutality of an egregious kind. But we do need to develop sensitivity towards the hidden and unexpected ways in which our rigid and placid four-part racial harmony can produce a certain closed-mindedness and intolerance that violate people's identities, communities, and prospects.

Instead, we should allow ourselves to appreciate the richness, beauty, and power of a social performance that contains polyphonic voices, discordant sounds, and even some wrong notes. We need this to transition from our hard yet brittle multiracialism to real social diversity, empathy, equality, creativity, and resilience, all necessary for surviving the radical disruptions of economic globalisation, technological transformation, and game-changing pandemics.

KENNETH PAUL TAN

Kenneth Paul Tan is a tenured Professor of Politics, Film, and Cultural Studies at Hong Kong Baptist University, which hired him under its Talent100 initiative in February 2021. Previously, he was a tenured Associate Professor at the National University of Singapore's (NUS) Lee Kuan Yew School of Public Policy (LKY School). He was Vice Dean of the LKY School during the most rapid and critical years of its growth and served in its senior leadership team for almost a decade. He has received numerous teaching awards over the years, including NUS's most prestigious Outstanding Educator Award. His books include *Singapore: Identity, Brand, Power* (Cambridge University Press, 2018), *Governing Global-City Singapore: Legacies and Futures After Lee Kuan Yew* (Routledge, 2017), *Cinema and Television in Singapore: Resistance in One Dimension* (Brill, 2008), and *Renaissance Singapore? Economy, Culture, and Politics* (NUS Press, 2007). He sits on the National Museum of Singapore's Advisory Board, chairs the Board of Directors of theatre company The Necessary Stage, and was the founding chair of the Asian Film Archive's Board of Directors.

The Question of "Chinese Privilege"

TAN CHEE LAY

I became a Chinese teacher of a junior college in Singapore in July 1998, and my very first school event was Racial Harmony Day, first commemorated by the Ministry of Education on 21 July that year. As a fresh-eyed teacher just starting out, I remembered memorising and delivering lectures in English from centrally produced notes on the infamous six-week race riots in 1964, which led to 36 deaths and over 500 injuries.

Of course, Racial Harmony Day has changed over the years, as it is now a celebration event in school, and even affectionately called RHD, with schools holding carnivals to creatively celebrate multiethnicity and values such as respecting differences and diversity.

However, even as the first batch of students who experienced RHD in school are into their forties today, we still see several racist incidents that went viral in 2021. Although the dire situations of the Covid-19 pandemic's Circuit Breaker and Safe Management Measures may have added to our social frustrations, did the twenty-odd years of education and "creative" celebrations of RHD not help to alleviate such racial problems, or even just lessen such tensions?

Is there "Chinese privilege"?
While we have always been reminded by politicians – and yes, by my own briefing notes for RHD too – that racial harmony is never a "natural state" or a "finished product", the hotly contested term in the 2021 sociopolitical discourse – "Chinese privilege" – still came as something of a surprise. Many Singaporeans could probably understand and accept that "Chinese privilege" is borrowed too loosely, even inconsiderately, from concepts of "white privilege" from the United States, but not too many can, or know how to, refute the fact that the privilege will exist as long as the Chinese are the majority in numbers.

Again, this is an overly simplistic perspective by merely judging from population proportion: Since Singapore's Chinese population is about 75%, so would there be a 75% chance that Chinese privilege takes place in society, or perhaps would Chinese residents have a 75% privilege?

This, of course, is illogical and unfounded. Although no one would attest to this specific percentage, a documentary on "Chinese privilege" produced by the main Chinese newspaper, *Lianhe Zaobao*, was nevertheless titled "Race and us – a 75% awkwardness". Chinese Singaporeans, of course, need not be socially awkward; they just have to live with this not easily modifiable majority percentage. Still, we have to ask: Was it just pure coincidence that in 2021's Covid-19 environment, a Chinese kicked an Indian woman in the chest and uttered racial slurs, another

The Question of "Chinese Privilege"

Chinese interrogated an inter-racial couple, demanding them to date within their respective races, and yet another Chinese hit a gong repeatedly to disrupt her Indian neighbour's prayer ritual?

Have we, the Chinese, been taking these mishaps for granted, or just waived them off as once-off incidents that were inapplicable to the majority of us? Then again, who is the majority of us? We must not forget that there is a huge group of Chinese-speaking (and especially Chinese dialect-speaking) Chinese who have felt disadvantaged ever since our society became more English-dominant. According to the 2020 National Census, we have 17.2% or over 500,000 Chinese who only speak Mandarin – which is not a small number at all. In fact, many of these Chinese speakers around me even laughed it off when they heard the term "Chinese privilege", citing all the injustices they endured over the years.

> **For the huge group of Chinese-speaking Chinese, the only privilege they could imagine is English language-privilege... their voices (in Chinese language or dialect) seemed to be muffled in our society where English has long become the lingua franca.**

These included the times when the language of instruction and assessment was changed from Chinese to English, when Chinese-medium schools were closed or transformed to English ones, when Nanyang University was merged with the University of Singapore to form the English-medium National University of Singapore, when all Chinese dialect programmes were banned on radio and TV, and when their English handicap resulted in grievances and lost opportunities.

Some even mentioned that they have never imagined, let alone heard, the term, and the only privilege they can imagine is English language-privilege. However, their voices (in Chinese language or dialect) seemed to be muffled in our society where English has long been the lingua franca. More importantly, they could consequently be the silent majority in this recent debate on "Chinese privilege", where we see many more news reports and forum letters in English than Chinese, especially in the virtual space – a Google search in both Chinese and English easily confirms this.

But in reality, when these Chinese speakers deny any Chinese privileges bestowed on them, contrary examples such as Special Assistance Plan (SAP) schools and the HDB Ethnic Integration Policy will be quickly brought up, and they may be further criticised as being chauvinistic and racism-blind, and, hence, wrongly accused a second time.

A stronger social fabric for more open discussions

More severe racial clashes than the recent incidents have taken place in Singapore's history, but those might just have been unreported in earlier times when social media didn't exist. I believe the seeming increase in racial disharmony incidents is partly due to the more reticent nature of the baby boomer generation, and partly due to the prowess of the Internet. While we should be careful not to over-generalise, "racial harmony" to our older generations (here I refer to those born before Singapore's independence) mostly means a deliberate avoidance of racial conflict and sensitive racial topics, even to the extent of being silent and indifferent.

The Question of "Chinese Privilege"

The same cannot be said for the younger generations, especially the Generations Y and Z (referring to those born after 1980), who are more outspoken, and willing to come forward to voice and share their experiences of racial disharmony, prejudice and conflict, which are not uncommon according to some online forums. Actually, there is a high possibility that the notion of "Chinese privilege" may be mostly prevalent amongst those from these younger generations, although their voices are notably much louder in social media and online forums.

There are probably more of us who have not lived in *kampongs*, or the old villages in the "good old days", than those who have. The *kampong* spirit, which includes racial harmony and a sense of community and solidarity, is probably less experienced by Singaporeans who grow up behind the closed doors of flats and private condominiums, in self-sufficiency and in the name of personal or family privacy.

One crucial drawback which results from a lack of a *kampong* community is the shortage of daily open interactions in a casual environment. Not only is this extremely critical in forging trusting relationships between different races, it would prevent the current state of long silence on sensitive racial topics from taking root. The avoidance of race-sensitive discussions by

The avoidance of race-sensitive discussions by the abovementioned older generations, as well as the indifference of younger generations due to less real-life interaction with other races in some cases, have unfortunately all contributed to the less-than-ideal racial situation we face today.

the abovementioned older generations, as well as the indifference of younger generations due to less real-life interaction with other races in some cases, have unfortunately all contributed to the less-than-ideal racial situation we face today.

A solution is certainly required, as we cannot just leave the problem as it is, hoping that it will improve with time. We have to solve it, and hopefully fast. Most critical of all, promoting open and empathetic talks and discussions on sensitive racial topics, even replacing certain misleading terms like "Chinese privilege" with "majority blind spots" (as suggested in public discussions) for more objective narratives, is desirable. Furthermore, discussions cannot just be restricted to like-minded people, especially of the same race, but with people from different ethnic groups, and from different walks of life. Yes, we may have progressed from the violent and tense racial riots of the 1960s, but the speed, reach and anonymity of social media pose newer and larger challenges to our nation's ongoing grapple with racism, and in our collective push for racial integration and harmony.

Despite such new challenges, we do now have a stronger social fabric than around the Independence period, due to years of National Education and Character and Citizenship Education (CCE) in schools, as well as stronger media publicity. Moreover, we have a common neutral language in English for the majority of citizens. Hence, the conditions for racial interactions and integration may actually be more positive and favourable than in most periods in the history of Singapore.

That said, much more can still be done in education and media publicity. The inclusiveness of SAP schools and even madrasahs can be further enhanced to strengthen multiracialism.

The Question of "Chinese Privilege"

The voices of other ethnic groups can be featured much more on TV and radio and in the press. Here, interpretation and translation of news, op-ed columns and other articles are some helpful avenues to better understand other races and the diverse opinions in our community.

Besides official multilingual programmes by the various ministries such as racial harmony events by the People's Association, other grassroots or bottom-up initiatives in society, such as the multilingual and multiracial Poetry Festival Singapore, where poets and audiences of different ethnic groups come together annually to celebrate poetry, can be further acknowledged and supported.

So today, twenty-odd years after I "lectured" on the first RHD, we have much more authentic materials, like the *Lianhe Zaobao* documentary, the numerous racist video clips, online forums and even this book of essays, to be used in future RHD celebrations. The less we shy away from these sensitive real-life racial issues and "majority blind spots", the more and better we can prepare our students and ourselves in the continuous quest for true and deep racial harmony. Besides aspiring, let's also take individual and collective steps towards a future in which Singaporeans of all ethnic groups can trustfully and confidently discuss, embrace and celebrate our racial diversity and unique differences.

Associate Professor Tan Chee Lay has lived in Singapore, Taiwan and the UK, and has studied Chinese Literature, English Studies and Business Administration. He completed his doctorate in Oriental Studies (Chinese literature) at St John's College, Cambridge University, specialising in Chinese poetry and poets in exile. He was awarded

TAN CHEE LAY

the Young Artist Award by the National Arts Council in 2004 and the Singapore Youth Award (Culture and the Arts), the highest accolade for youth, in 2006. A former tutor of the Chinese Language Elective Programme, he is currently Deputy Head of the Asian Languages and Cultures Academic Group at the National Institute of Education, Nanyang Technological University. An award-winning artist, calligrapher and writer, he has published and edited over 20 creative writing and academic books.

12

Deep Roots, Verdant Leaves: Inspirations from Sinophone Singapore

TAN DAN FENG

In the field of translation, to which I have devoted 30 years of my life, there is a well-known Italian saying: "*traduttore, traditore*", which translates literally as: "translator, traitor". Some interpret this adage to mean that no translation can ever be completely true to the original, since linguistic and cultural differences inevitably distort any attempt at reproduction. Others see this proverb as a warning of the unavoidable plight that befalls translators – namely, that they can never truly belong to any one community, tainted as they are by their intimate knowledge of another language and culture. Can one ever be certain of the allegiance of someone who serves two masters?

This predicament of being "caught between cultures" is something many Singaporeans will be familiar with. Told that they should value and celebrate their ancestral roots, while, at the same time, be active participants in a modern, multicultural nation, they exist in a perpetual state of tension and quest for the perfect balance that would insulate them from accusations of cultural insularity at one end, and being shallow imitators of the West at the other. The late theatre doyen and cultural theorist Kuo Pao Kun – in the book *Images at the Margins: A Collection of Kuo Pao Kun's Plays (1983–1992)* – coined the term "cultural orphans" to describe this state of existence:

> At the confluence of several great civilisations and in the international flow of information, Singaporeans sense the richness of interacting with every place but also feel the pain and frustration of not belonging anywhere. Boundless space, boundless bewilderment, boundless loss and boundless hope – there naturally emerges an orphan mentality and a condition of marginality. Even if we were able to trace back and return to our respective cultural parentages, we would still not be at home in the past. The orphan can only grope for a way forward, to make his or her own spiritual home in the midst of loss and alienation.

This mentality, no doubt, is a characteristic of most immigrant societies, but the prominence of ethnic and linguistic categories in the management of Singapore society in crucial areas such as education and community support accentuates its impact. In local media, exhortations to stay vigilant against acts of ethnic chauvinism alternate with calls for more to be done to arrest the decline of mother tongues and cultures, a constant reminder of the perpetual (and colossal) effort required to uphold both parts of the phrase, "unity in diversity".

How Singapore's Chinese "cultural orphans" reached out to other cultures

The question of how a society comprising different cultures could become "one united people" was very much on the minds of the early Singapore Chinese intellectual community. Over a century ago, Khoo Seok Wan, the highly influential man of letters and leader of the Teochew community, had already penned a poem incorporating transliterated Malay words (*makan*, *mabok*, *mari*, *main*, *sama*) within a classical Chinese seven-character quatrain form. Playing on the Chinese character "马" (*ma*, horse), he ends with the entreaty: "何妨三马吃同槽" (may all three horses eat from the same trough), in which he offers the reader three possible, but complementary, interpretations of the word "三马" (*sanma*): (a) a literal translation, that is, "three horses"; (b) a transliteration of the Malay word "*sama*" (same); and, (c) a metaphorical description of the three major Malayan ("马") ethnic groups. The poem certainly qualifies as one of the earliest Singapore literary works on racial harmony.

Several decades later, the campaign to develop and champion a distinctive Malayan Chinese literary form unique to the region gained momentum. Major literary pioneers such as Miao Xiu and Zhao Rong consciously injected their works of fiction with vernacular colloquialisms drawn from the languages of daily Singapore life, including Hokkien, Cantonese, Hakka, Malay and English. The major debate among Singapore Chinese writers over establishing a form of Chinese literature specific to their new homeland and separate from other parts of the Sinophone world extended over several years, leaving a valuable record of how the local Chinese engaged with the issue of evolving identities as they deepened their roots in multicultural Singapore. Proficient and comfortable in their ancestral language and culture, the writers nevertheless recognised the need to actively adapt to find common ground with the other communities on the island.

> "The higher you reach into the respective cultures, the more you see all the branches and leaves touching each other. But the stalk, the stem, the trunk are very separated. This is where our level of art is – they are very separated. But if you go deeper, the roots touch."
> – Kuo Pao Kun

Such efforts among the Chinese-speaking intelligentsia continued in the fledgling years of self-governance. Nanyang University, then the first Chinese-medium institution of higher learning outside China, also became a stronghold for the promotion of Malay language and culture. Graduates of Nanyang University, such as Liaw Yock Fang, Yang Quee Yee and Leo Suryadinata, subsequently went on to make their mark in the fields of Malay language translation, literature, publishing, lexicography and education. Motivating them was the belief that they needed to move beyond their own community to find solidarity with their fellow citizens through the National Language.

Indeed, Malay literary giant Usman Awang alludes to this solidarity in his poem "Pemuda dan Gadis Tionghoa" (Young Chinese Men and Women), which is addressed to Lim Huan Boon

Inspirations from Sinophone Singapore

and Goh Choo Keng, students of Malay at Nanyang University, and Linda Chen, who was studying at the University of Malaya. The poem – from the book *Sahabatku: Puisi-puisi 5 Bahasa* (My Friend: Poetry translated into 5 languages) – starts with these lines:

> (Kong Hee Fatt Choy to Lim, Goh and Linda)
> The sweet tomorrow in our nation's history
> fills the faces of young Chinese men and women
> having grown up together with trees of a fertile earth
> rubber shoots and farmland under the eastern sun.
> From your first cry when you were born here
> till your last breath
> sing our beloved national song with conviction
> together we will feel the new pain of a freed country.

Looking back at the literary and intellectual history of the Chinese-speaking community in Singapore, one can see that there has always been a recognition of the benefits of multiculturalism and the necessity of accommodation to seek unity of purpose and common cause with other communities. In an interview conducted in the 1990s – published in the book *9 Lives: 10 Years of Singapore Theatre (1987–1997)* – Kuo Pao Kun gives an eloquent description of multiculturalism:

> Biculturally or multiculturally… the higher you reach into the respective cultures, the more you see all the branches and leaves touching each other. But the stalk, the stem, the trunk are very separated. This is where our level

of art is — they are very separated. But if you go deeper, the roots touch. You go higher, the branches touch, the leaves touch. And of course, the cross-pollination is done up there. And you absorb the same nutrients, deep underneath. And this is the beauty of multiculturalism.

I often use this passage in my lectures on literary translation and intercultural communication. The mention of roots offers an important reminder that every human being, irrespective of background, finds nourishment and sustenance in the same things, while the description of branches and leaves emphasises how we have to always strive to grow and reach greater heights to reap the advantages of diversity.

How to grow new roots, towards a truer, richer multiculturalism

Over the years, I have begun looking for other analogies for what it means to be "multicultural". It was during my research on Han Wai Toon, one of the more fascinating figures in Singapore's intellectual history, that I found inspiration. Han had come to Singapore from Hainan Island as a penniless young man in 1915. Despite having only a basic education, he eventually found a job at Medical Office, a private pharmacy started by German immigrants, where he later rose to become a shareholder, acquiring a formidable knowledge of chemistry and other sciences along the way. An active supporter and member of scholarly organisations in Singapore, he was close to the leading Chinese intellectual and cultural figures of the day, including luminaries such as Xu Beihong and Yu Dafu.

Gaining renown as a global expert on Chinese ceramics, he was held in high esteem even by the colonial intellectual elite, who nominated him for membership in the prestigious Oriental Ceramics Society in London. Later, he received a personal invitation from Guo Moruo, then president of the Chinese Academy of Sciences, to take a full-time position as consultant to the Palace Museum in Beijing, where he spent the last seven years of his life.

Seen through today's lens, Han was a rare and true early Singapore "bicultural", who gained admission into the sanctums of culture in both London and Beijing. But what makes his achievements all the more incredible (and which brings to mind Kuo's analogy of branches and roots) is the fact that he never learned to speak English or Mandarin, communicating only in his native Hainanese, Hokkien and Malay.

> **Perhaps successful multiculturalism requires every citizen to make a conscious decision to be "inarched" to a new culture, acquiring additional sets of roots that will continue to grow together with the original, to nourish and enrich the multicultural soul, just like what the local Chinese writers and Nanyang University students attempted to do in earlier times.**

On his departure to Beijing in 1962, members of the Chinese culturati in Singapore presented Han with a Chinese painting by renowned local artist Lim Mu Hue, depicting him and his intellectual friends relaxing in his rambutan plantation along Upper Thomson Road. Han had acquired the plantation, which he named "Garden of Foolish Indulgences", as a place for the literati and artists to gather for scholarly discussions, but the plantation was also commercially successful due to scientific farming methods Han introduced. Fruit vendors in Geylang were willing to pay more for his higher-quality rambutans, and some of his trees, which bore multi-flavoured fruit, drew curious visitors.

It was when scrutinising a photograph of this painting that I noticed the irregular look of some of the trees. Unlike regular plants where a single stem extends from the soil before separating into branches, these trees looked as though their stems were perched on converging tentacles emerging from the ground, before separating into branches again. It was when I checked a textbook on botany that I realised that these trees were products of a process called "inarch grafting" (or "inarching").

Unlike conventional grafting, where a shoot is severed from its parent plant and joined to the stem of a different plant, eventually taking on its characteristics, inarch grafting conjoins two (or more) adjacent plants with intact root systems, allowing the new entity to simultaneously possess multiple parent stocks. The result is a plant that is sturdier and healthier, and less prone to genetic deficiencies and other damage. All of the roots continue to grow even as the now-improved plant retains the positive characteristics of each parent. It was through inarch grafting that Han could grow his famous rambutan trees that bore delicious fruit of different characteristics on different branches. One report cited a tree that produced seven different flavours of rambutan fruit.

As a translator and someone who navigates cultures, this horticultural concept strikes me as a fitting metaphor for what it means to be multicultural. Rather than waiting for nature to bring about cross-pollination as Kuo suggests, perhaps successful multiculturalism requires every citizen to make a conscious decision to be "inarched" to a new culture, acquiring additional sets of roots that will continue to grow together with the original, to nourish and enrich the multicultural soul, just like what the local Chinese writers and Nanyang University students attempted to do in earlier times.

A top-down and mechanistic approach is no longer sufficient to deal with the pliable and complex nature of human culture and identity, especially as Singapore moves from the bread-and-butter concerns of a developing nation to the higher aspirations of an affluent society. Perhaps it is time for a change in mindset, where the emphasis shifts from defining categories to encouraging deeper roots and higher branches irrespective of category, creating a verdant canopy that benefits the entire forest. Perhaps this is the path to achieving the lofty aspiration of "one united people".

Tan Dan Feng began his career as a translator in 1992. He was director of Select Books and co-founded The Select Centre, a not-for-profit organisation shortlisted for the London Book Fair International Excellence Awards for Best Literary Translation Initiative. His edited works include *Singapore Shifting Boundaries: Social Change in the Early 21st Century* (Asian Urban Lab, 2011) and *Living in Babel: Singapore Literature in Translation* (Canopy, 2017). His latest published translation is *Memorandum: A Sinophone Singaporean Short Story Reader* (Ethos Books, 2020). He is currently based in Canada.

"Same Same, but Different": The Peranakan Experience of a Multiracial Singapore

LINDA CHEE

You can call me Ms One-United-People. That's me, even before I was born.

I am 66.5% Chinese, 27.5% Malay and 6.0% Indian. This is scientifically proven, from a blood sampling done in 2018 by the Genome Institute of Singapore (GIS) to determine the DNA profile of the Peranakans in Singapore.

It was a revelation that startled me. A pleasant one, though, to discover that I have Indian blood. And to know I have an unexpectedly high percentage of Malay genes. The Peranakan Chinese tested in the GIS study showed an average of 5.6% Malay ancestry. Incidentally, the CMIO (Chinese-Malay-Indian-Others) silos of the Singapore population census in June 2020 are recorded as 76.2% Chinese, 15.0% Malay and 7.4% Indian.

The GIS finding confirmed what I had always thought: that I was not totally Chinese. I recall wondering why I could not

"Same Same, but Different": The Peranakan Experience

state "Straits Chinese" as my race when I turned 12 years old in 1969 and earned my own pink identity card as a Singapore citizen. After all, I proudly belong to a community of Peranakan Chinese, in which the men are referenced as Baba and the women as Nyonya. We had an illustrious family history as British subjects in the Straits Settlements and we could speak English fluently.

When I was a child, none of my relatives spoke Mandarin or Chinese dialects within the family. The food we enjoyed, like spicy *sambal belacan*, *buah keluak* and *kelo* curries, was not the typical Chinese fare. Everyday meals were partaken with our fingers, not with cutlery or chopsticks. Quite a few of my uncles and aunts had noticeably Malay or Eurasian features. My mother wore the *sarong* at home daily. When she dressed up for special occasions, she looked beautiful in her embroidered *sarong kebaya* and dazzling Peranakan jewellery.

Our houses were furnished with ornately carved sideboards that displayed colourful Nyonya ware and heavy blackwood mother-of-pearl furniture which were popular among the Peranakans. Our albums of black-and-white photographs showed the lavish lifestyles of past generations. My forebears, as I discovered, were merchants who had ventured out of China as early as the 1600s to make their fortunes in the Malay Archipelago. After settling down in Melaka for over 10 generations, there was bound to be some mixing with local Malay women, although there was no proof in our patrilineal family records of any unions with non-Chinese females.

My two older brothers and I grew up speaking Baba Malay with our parents, both of whom were Peranakans and were not literate in the Chinese language. The Melaka Baba Malay is a unique blend of Malay, Indonesian and Hokkien dialect, with a sprinkling of Portuguese, Dutch, Indian languages and whatever port city-speak that our ancestors had mixed into our largely conversational vernacular.

Ironically for me, studying standard Malay as a second language was a torture as I spoke only Baba Malay outside school. I was just so glad I had a choice not to study Chinese, which was dreaded by many. I only came to realise in the last 20 years or so that the Malay language is very different, in spelling, intonation and syntax, from Baba Malay. This was after I joined The Peranakan Association Singapore to rediscover my roots. I was understandably perplexed, not knowing which words belonged where.

Most fortunately, as a student, I qualified to study at the local university in 1976 even though I failed my Malay A-levels. It was a huge relief because, barely a few years later, the national bilingual policy meant that one could not enter university without passing a second-language exam. Looking back now, being a graduate and proficient in the English language not only directed my career path, but also shaped my life and relationships outside my family. Many of my Peranakan Chinese peers who had similar experiences went on to excel in the English literary arts.

Chinese, but not Chinese?

Being a Chinese who can converse well in colloquial Malay helps to open doors in daily life, like when I am buying Malay food or speaking the language with Malay friends. This makes me feel good. It is also useful when driving up to Malaysia and touring Indonesia. But Chinese-speaking activities are out of the way for

"Same Same, but Different": The Peranakan Experience

me because I do not understand the language. Not learning Chinese from young makes learning formidable as an adult, especially with the tonal subtleties that can change a friendly greeting to an expletive.

Growing up in post-colonial Singapore, I managed to pick up a smattering of rudimentary Hokkien from my largely Hokkien-speaking neighbours in a village called Kampong San Teng along Upper Thomson Road. My paternal grandfather in Melaka had sent my father to Singapore to manage a rubber plantation off Island Club Road and other properties for his good friend. Ours was the only Peranakan family in that village. Somehow, we managed to communicate with our Chinese neighbours in pasar, or bazaar, Malay.

> **Hawkers belittled me, as my ragged Hokkien did not pass muster. The remarks were hurtful. The term OCBC or Orang Cina Bukan Cina ("Chinese people who are not Chinese") emerged to label our Peranakan community.**

I felt most acutely an outcast when I accompanied my mother to the big wet market at Tekka on Sundays. The hawkers spoke dialect to me and I was often belittled as my ragged Hokkien did not pass muster. The remarks were hurtful. Many Nyonyas and Babas faced a similar predicament. This was how the term *Orang Cina Bukan Cina* ("Chinese people who are not Chinese" in Malay), shortened to "OCBC", also the acronym of a well-known local bank, emerged to label our Peranakan community.

Such sentiments influenced the circle of friends I made, who were more comfortable speaking English, and the music and television shows we switched on. I grew up on a diet of music that my father loved, from Mantovani and Matt Monro to the Ray Conniff Singers. My brothers and I preferred the Bee Gees to Teresa Teng, the Andy Williams Show to Wang Sa and Ye Fong. Such different worlds.

Despite our wide exposure to Western culture and thought, I was recently reminded of the declaration made in 1939 by my Melaka-born paternal great-grandfather Tan Jin Ann, as captured in our family genealogy book: "We are Chinese and must not forget that we are such, and that we are always to be Chinese in the real sense of the word." I am now in my 60s and proudly heed his words in appreciation of our deep-seated cultural values such as respect for my parents and elders, and upholding traditions during occasions such as the Lunar New Year.

But does blood matter in multiracial Singapore?

In 2005, my husband Colin and I celebrated our silver wedding anniversary with over 200 of our relatives and friends. The joyous Peranakan-themed evening rounded off with many getting up from their seats to *joget*, a traditional dance. One of our American guests, Phil Wetz, remarked that he could never forget the sight of people of so many races in one room, all having a good time: Singaporeans who are Chinese, Malay, Indian and Eurasian together with our Australian, American, Hongkonger friends and more.

A year ago, I emailed Phil a photo of himself at the dinner, for old times' sake. Again, he mentioned that remarkable experience of togetherness amongst people of different appearances and nationalities. How we have taken moments like these for granted! It took a foreigner to make me realise that beyond DNA,

"Same Same, but Different": The Peranakan Experience

multiracialism has been ingrained in me as a Singaporean since I was very young.

Back in 1963, when I attended primary school at the now-defunct Sembawang Hills Estate School, we were never taught to differentiate by race or religion. My principal was dear Mr D'Silva and my Primary One teacher was a lovely Chinese lady called Mrs Bull who I believe was married to an Indian. I sat between a Malay boy and a Chinese girl in the front row because we were about the same height then, and I was short-sighted.

The first song I learned in school was "Rain, Rain Go Away". I also sang "Mary Had a Little Lamb" and "London Bridge is Falling Down". As little children from the *kampongs*, we had seen neither lambs nor London, but we knew these delightful English ditties by heart. I also remember singing a Jewish folk song, *Hava Nagila* ("Let Us Rejoice"), at a school concert performance.

All through secondary school at Raffles Girls' to National Junior College, my friends and I were never curious about where our parents came from, or their social backgrounds. There was a girl surnamed Lee who looked totally English, but her father was Chinese. It did not matter. We were colour-blind as friends.

Strength in diversity: Reclaiming Peranakan heritage

In the last 10 years or so, when people in their 50s tend to start thinking of gatherings to reminisce about our school days, it struck me that some of my CMIO classmates, interestingly, were actually of Arab, Ceylonese, Parsi or Gujarati descent, or from a host of other ancestries. Going to the same school, sharing at mealtimes, sports, games, studying and laughing together, we were comfortable with one another, in Singapore.

What brought us together? A common language – English – in an open society. English has been the greatest gift of Britannia, the erstwhile British Empire, to the world. To Singapore, it is the lifeblood that connects us locally and globally.

I am certainly not alone in being thankful to our late founding father, Mr Lee Kuan Yew, for his vision and foresight to legislate English as the main working language. And for his policy of education for all. As a girl I would not have had access to a good education all the way to university, and to a good career as a working mother, if not for Mr Lee.

Then again, something has had to give. I have "paid the price" for focusing on English and disregarding much of my Peranakan heritage until about 20 years back, as mentioned earlier. I had become *karat*, or "rusty", in the use of Baba Malay, my mother tongue, the language I grew up speaking. And with that, a large part of passing on my culture to my two children. It had been de-emphasised with the constant stress on their having to pass their second language, Chinese, or else be held back.

But with my two grandsons, aged two and five, events have proved to be a homecoming of sorts. To my surprise, their parents are now more keen for them to pick up Baba Malay from me. It is their cultural heritage, they say, which proudly differentiates them from other Singaporeans. Same same, but different, eh? We were amused one day when the Malay nursery teacher said the younger grandson processes and responds faster when spoken to in Malay.

My daily life is a constant reminder of the ebb and flow of differences yet similarities in my encounters and experiences.

Colin and I go for strength training once a week to tone our

"Same Same, but Different": The Peranakan Experience

muscles. It is a pain prevention strategy in our ageing process. The instructors and their clients in the gym are like the United Nations. We train under a very experienced young instructor called Bronwen Appel. Where is she from? "I'm Singaporean!" she grins brightly. Born in South Africa, her whole family chose to become naturalised citizens after being permanent residents for many years here since she was a young girl. Her sister is married to a Welsh-Indian Singaporean and their children go to a Singaporean kindergarten in their HDB *kampong*.

> **Our differences and varied cultures have made us coherent as a country, and given us a unique identity which, in itself, is a cause to celebrate our unity.**

Such diversity in Singapore, I feel, is our strength – a trait to be accepted, valued and enjoyed. Our differences and varied cultures have made us coherent as a country, and given us a unique identity which, in itself, is a cause to celebrate our unity.

I look forward to Singapore's colourful and vibrant future, in more ways than one. As is often heard, New Zealand has more sheep than people. Singapore has more trees than people – nearly 8 million trees cooling 6 million people in our "City in a Garden", now becoming a "City in Nature". We have our Merlion, Gardens by the Bay, our unique lingo like *lah*, *shiok*, *siao* and *sotong*, our work ethic, discipline in a pandemic, marvellous food... and much more. We are unique in ourselves.

Life will never be perfect. Cynics may scoff but, to me, blood does not matter as a Singaporean. Mutual respect does. And shared values of equality, humility, harmony and peace in a multicultural society.

LINDA CHEE

This is my *kampong* that I grew up in, identify with, and proudly stand for, as a Singaporean.

Cheers to my beloved country, our little island in the sun.

Linda Chee is a second-generation Singaporean, the daughter of Peranakan Chinese parents with roots dating back more than 10 generations in Melaka, Malaysia. Linda was formerly a journalist with the *Business Times* before she moved on to corporate life 30 years ago to find out what actually happens on the other side of the fence. She is the editor of *The Peranakan* magazine, a role she has helmed for 13 years to proudly promote the community's rich cultural heritage. This publication is the flagship of the 2,000-strong The Peranakan Association Singapore (TPAS). Linda is married to Colin Chee, the current president of TPAS, whose Peranakan forebears were from Sarawak.

Towards a More Conscious and Inclusive Capitalism

JOYCE LIM

The colourful Peranakan '70s
Growing up in the 1970s in a Peranakan family, I lived a fairly protected life. Outside of attending classes at Methodist Girls School, going to church on Sundays at the local Anglican church, music lessons and weekend swims at the club, there wasn't much else I was allowed to do. I never took the bus till I was in secondary school, never wandered beyond the watchful, guarding eyes of my *majie* (a Cantonese term for "nanny"), and never passed Mandarin as a mother tongue. This was just how it was.

I grew up surrounded by loud songs, soups and *sambal* spice. My mother – an émigré who moved from Sabah to Singapore in the '40s – insisted that we all had a wicked brew of herbal soup at every meal. Soupy rice, she calls it – right till today. My father, a booming, loud and fiercely expressive gentleman, was Peranakan in every way. Right till the year he passed away, he established that life would not be worth living without *sambal belacan* and *keroncong*, a '60s folkstyle music popular at that time amongst Peranakans.

I grew up not recognising racial tensions. My best friend in primary school was an Indian girl. We innocently imitated our Indian teachers who spoke with an unmistakable accent. All the teachers had nicknames. We were in the arts stream in our secondary years, and despite being the worst class in the best school, we had loads of fun. Life was colourful.

The turbulent '60s of racial tensions

I never saw the race riots of 1964 which marked the beginning of the end of Singapore's place in the Federation of Malaysia in 1965.

A former People's Action Party Cabinet minister, Othman Wok (1924–2017), recounted in his book, *Never in My Wildest Dreams*, that in early July 1964, Syed Jaffar Albar – then Secretary-General of Malaysia's United Malays National Organisation (UMNO) – accused Malay PAP members in Singapore of being "un-Islamic, anti-Islam, anti-Malay and traitors to their own community" at a mass rally. He declared that "Malays in Singapore have long been oppressed", and urged that "Malays must unite to defend their own interest".

Mahathir Mohamad, who later served as UMNO Chairman, wrote in his memoirs that the "Chinese in Singapore, being mostly wealthy, were not used to the ways of the Malays. They knew them only as servants and members of the poor labouring class of Singapore. By looking down on the Malays, they may have also underestimated the community's strength."

As Singapore's founding Prime Minister Lee Kuan Yew reflected in his memoirs: "It was impossible to dispel or overcome the deep-seated distrust evoked once irrational killing had been prompted simply by the mere appearance, whether Malay or Chinese, of the victim."

Othman Wok argued that one of the causes of the 1964 riots was the lack of understanding between ethnic groups because they lived in separate areas. By 1969, the Singapore government began to address this with a Housing and Development Board (HDB) rehousing scheme, placing Singaporeans of different ethnicities side-by-side together in public dwellings, with the aim of promoting understanding and respect for each other's culture and lifestyle.

My perspective is that the key factor is not racial tensions per se that exist in Singapore, but a gap between the haves and have-nots.

Such increased intercommunal ties disincentivised ethnic violence. Today, Singaporeans live and work amidst racial harmony.

Racial conflict today: Has the world gone crazy?

When a Chinese man blatantly made racist remarks against an interracial couple along Singapore's Orchard Road in 2020, Law and Home Affairs Minister K. Shanmugam commented: "I used to believe that Singapore was moving in the right direction on racial tolerance and harmony. Based on recent events, I am not so sure anymore."

On the other side of the globe, Americans of the '60s saw protests against racial segregation, discrimination in employment, housing, transportation, and commerce, fuelled by the growth of the civil rights movement. This pattern of protests would be repeated several times over the next decade as Americans energised the Black Power movements of the '70s.

In 1992, mass protests and riots exploded in Los Angeles after the Rodney King case. Twenty years later, activists in America loosely banded together in the Black Lives Matter movement, founded in response to the acquittal of a white man who fatally shot an unarmed 17-year-old black student who was visiting relatives in a Florida gated community.

America's recent uprisings resemble those of 1919, 1943 and 1968 in that they grew out of simmering hatred seeded by the long, festering history of white violence and police brutality against African-Americans, which claim hundreds of lives every year.

But this is not just a black-and-white affair. Today's demonstrations are noticeably interracial, with African-American, Asian-American, Latino and white faces appearing in city centres, obstructing bridges and highways, and gathering in front of the White House. This suggests a new phase of opposition that is uniting groups who historically did not share any commonalities. Where conflicts have erupted, those assaulted, tear-gassed, or shot with rubber bullets are of all races.

While clashes of the past happened mostly in black neighbourhoods, today they have often started in wealthy downtowns and suburban shopping malls. Amidst soaring unemployment and ongoing racial injustice in America, we see an amalgamation of both old and new.

Today's protesters exploit past incidents of bloodshed and rampage to demand sweeping reforms. George Floyd's death in 2020 has sparked a global movement, with statues of slave owners

Towards a More Conscious and Inclusive Capitalism

being torn down from Bristol, England, to Richmond, Virginia.

Just looking at these two differing scenarios – one in Singapore where a Chinese man makes racial accusations against an Indian man, and the other in America with the Black Lives Matter protests and demonstrations – there are marked differences.

Racial disparities in Singapore fuel a call for solidarity against individuals who sow hatred for others, denting the core of becoming one united people regardless of race, language or religion.

In America, it seems that one racial event that gets public attention can trigger a chain of reactions around the country, partly motivated by longstanding, deep-seated anger.

No matter how you look at it, racial aberrations do exist, be it overt or covert. In Singapore, we tend to address the core of the issue at hand – why it happened and what we need to do to stop it. At some stage, it seems to point back to the perpetrator having some kind of mental challenge; as in the case of Tan Beow Hiong. Tan made headlines in Singapore in 2021 for harassing random passengers on the public transport system, making derogatory remarks about them and posting videos on YouTube that incited racial prejudices. The court sent her for psychiatric observation.

Revamping the old "five Cs": Bridging the elitist gap

Racial identity is constructed, then reconstructed, by individuals in the presence of others, implied, imagined and real. The process of constructing a racial identity has been described by the Stanford University social psychologist Hazel Rose Markus as: "You think therefore I am", a twist on the 17th-century French philosopher René Descartes' famous statement.

My perspective is that the key factor is not racial tensions per se in Singapore, but a gap between the haves and have-nots. I was in my prime earning years when the "5Cs" were all the rage — driving a nice car, living in a high-rise condo, spending on seemingly limitless credit cards, toting around wads of cash, and spending weekends at the country club. We aspired, and competed, to acquire all these material luxuries.

Embarrassingly, I participated in this drive for the ultimate Singaporean lifestyle, only to seek the intangibles later on in life. My collection of Cs has shifted towards developing culture, care for self and others, a deeper commitment to purpose and fulfilment, and contributing to make a difference where I can best add value.

No matter how you look at it, there is always a hierarchy, an internal mechanism that tells you that you're not good enough compared to others. Expand this thinking beyond your peripheral vision and you'll see that it's not that much different between technologies, countries and economies. This spirit of competition breeds a combative, fighting attitude that spurs creativity to new heights. Major world powers and their space programmes are competing to see who can get everyone to Mars first. After that, what's next? The rat race will always continue; just make sure you're on top of the food chain.

"Beingness": Trusting the environment

How we grow up plays an important part in creating our state of existence in this world, or what is known as our "beingness".

When I was 20, I moved to the US to work, but I never felt belittled or victimised from racism. From the US, I moved to Australia for a one-year work assignment; it was in Sydney, while I was crossing the road, that some youths stuck their head out of a car and shouted: "Go home, Chink!" The elitist in me brushed it off as a consequence of their lack of education.

Growing up in Singapore, I learnt how to build a strong trust with the environment. Is this a bad thing? I don't think so. I am an urban dweller. I have travelled extensively for work, and lived in the West for over 15 years. After a while, I find that all cities can offer a personal space for living, and a respite from "real life", with the climate, environment and attitudes being the only differences between them. But at the core, the world is increasingly being perceived as one planet, and we are all mere pawns in a game much bigger than our insignificant egos.

Step into the void, towards inclusiveness

In today's world, in which volatility, uncertainty, chaos and ambiguity are new norms, individuals are progressively overwhelmed as they navigate stress related to work and play. The Covid-19 crisis has delivered some valuable life lessons. Home-based learning has forced parents with young children to pivot between online classes, zoom meetings and entertaining bored kids at home. It is multitasking at a new level. A notification from the health ministry on a possible Covid-19 contamination then implies an entire medical protocol to follow, requiring a level of responsibility and discipline to self-quarantine, self-test and report.

While the Singapore government has provided emergency funding to support small and medium-sized organisations which have been affected by the pandemic, the handout programmes will eventually come to an end. Companies must transform their businesses, or stay stuck in the same conundrum.

Action creates change. It is the only path to success. Even if you're on the right track, you'll get run over if you just sit there, waiting for life to happen. We can only progress. The speed of change is accelerating at a pace that is so fast, yet slow in current time. This means that if we are unable to pivot and adapt, communicate and collaborate, we will find ourselves forgotten, declared irrelevant and archaic.

I think it's great that the Singapore government champions the evolution of a lifelong learning culture that meets the demands of a dynamic future. This plants a seed of a learning imperative that nurtures an environment stimulating personal and professional development and growth.

> **To truly live a future in which Singaporeans are one united people takes a level of conscious capitalism – a socially responsible economic and political philosophy that requires reinvention at the highest level.**

To truly live a future in which Singaporeans are one united people takes a level of conscious capitalism – a socially responsible economic and political philosophy that requires reinvention at the highest level. Reinventive models of cooperation that have the speed, scale and impact of transformational change can only come together with deep purposeful collaboration.

This means that cross-sectoral, public-and-private partnerships across all sectors of non-government organisations, governments, civil society and academic organisations need to join forces to leverage each sector's strengths and expertise, collectively boosting expectations and making a difference where it counts the most. Grouping along racial lines has no place in this future, and

Towards a More Conscious and Inclusive Capitalism

working alone will no longer cut it. Being responsible and choosing to lead is the only way up.

If anything, Singaporeans, because of their multiracial heritage and history, are well-placed to be leading examples of such an inclusive society. We just need the courage to reinvent policies, quieten some old thoughts, and be willing to bury old habits. After all, living an inspired life is way more fun, and much more colourful.

Joyce Lim is a marketer, adult educator, consultant and producer. She holds a PhD in leadership and completed an MBA in Global Business focused on corporate social responsibility during the pandemic lockdown. A creative catalyst, she spent much of her career in regional marketing with brands including Cirque du Soleil, Disney, Esplanade Theatres and World Expo. She has produced and directed hundreds of live events and led over 200 leadership seminars and training sessions in the Asia-Pacific region.

15

The Sooner, the Better: Fighting a Different Virus of Racial Tensions

BILLY STEVEN TAY

Growing up, you're taught the National Pledge in the four languages: English, Malay, Chinese and Tamil. You'd mix around with friends from all races, try different cuisines in the school canteen and wear different costumes to school on Racial Harmony Day. At least, that's what I did.

You'd head home to your neighbourhood. You've got neighbours of different races living near you. You'd sit down and turn on the television. A local sitcom comes on, and there's a family from each race, all living harmoniously in the same neighbourhood and estate.

Since independence, Singapore has always reiterated the importance of racial relations in our society. After all, it was race riots and racial tensions that caused our split from Malaya in 1965 – and subsequently, our development of values that shaped Singapore's unique blend of multiculturalism and multiracialism.

Fighting a Different Virus of Racial Tensions

These values were taught in school and inculcated in everyone from a young age. Such values were also reflected in the media and through policies. Have neighbours of all races living on your floor? It isn't by chance; it's a product of the Housing and Development Board's ethnic quota policy to prevent racial enclaves from forming. Through policies, rules, and law and order, the omnipresence of racial harmony has been prevalent in Singapore society since the beginning. And if you don't agree with them, laws are in place to keep you in check.

As unique as Singapore's approach to ensuring harmony is, it has come with a lot of sacrifices. For one, freedom of speech is heavily curtailed, especially when it comes to making controversial jokes that border on casual racism, perpetuating stereotypes for the sake of jokes and politically incorrect commentary. However, on the other side of the globe, things aren't perfect either.

Take a look at the United States, for example. Despite inroads in race relations and the Civil Rights Movement, many African-Americans still face discrimination, police brutality and racial profiling. Such problems are exacerbated by the freedom to own firearms and weapons – this is when discrimination becomes violence, when violence turns to tragedy. Without hardline laws in place, it's up to the people to fight for their rights. Movements such as Black Lives Matter saw people around the country marching in protest, in support of the rights of African-Americans.

Meanwhile, it's illegal to hold an assembly in Singapore without a permit. 'Nuff said. Singaporeans are put in an odd situation here – those who want to publicly fight for what they believe in are largely sidelined by the law, left to depend on the law to keep things in order. Perhaps this has contributed to the touchiness of racial issues and the avoidance of discussing such matters, lest there are repercussions from the said laws, or even public naming and shaming.

Why we now need difficult conversations about race
An Indian man rings a bell as part of a Hindu prayer ritual. He's done so for the past 20 years. His neighbour exits her flat and starts hitting a handheld gong. With each successive hit, she gets louder and faster, drowning out the sound of his bell. She walks back to her flat, vexed and infuriated.

A Chinese man confronts a younger Indian man along Orchard Road about having a Chinese girlfriend. He tells them that they should date people of their own race. The Indian man calls him a racist. The Chinese man agrees, and accuses him of preying on Chinese girls.

As unique as Singapore's approach to ensuring harmony is, it came with a lot of sacrifices. For one, freedom of speech is heavily curtailed, especially when it comes to making controversial jokes that border on casual racism, perpetuating stereotypes for the sake of jokes and politically incorrect commentary.

Throughout the Covid-19 pandemic, we've seen a troubling trend emerge: constant finger-pointing, blaming and discrimination aimed at certain ethnic groups.

We came to know of those aforementioned incidents through social media and online newsfeeds. Gone are the days of people hearing things through the grapevine and by word-of-mouth; all it takes now is two taps on a screen to disrupt our cohesion: one tap to record, one tap to upload. Even as a 19-year-old, I've already seen countless immature opinions being thrown into cyberspace without a care in the world, by both teens and adults.

Peers older than me often remark how lucky they were that social media had yet to come into existence when they were tweens, lest it document the pitfalls of their immaturity growing up. That some things are better left unsaid has never rung truer. Observers will turn into commenters, firing their own racially charged opinions and beliefs from behind a screen, adding fuel to the fire.

The pandemic has brought stress, anxiety and uncertainty. More often than not, it has tested our unity as a country and our racial and religious harmony. Some in the Malay community saw red when the government announced Covid-19 measures just before the Hari Raya Puasa holiday, and questioned why the government appeared to be more lax when it was Chinese New Year earlier in the year. Just a coincidence, or a bias?

In the days of normalcy before the pandemic, we had the emotional capacity and habit to keep and maintain a sense of harmony. But with Covid-19 looming over our physical and mental health, our minds weren't preoccupied with maintaining harmony – they were replaced with worry about the virus changing our lives for the worse. Some of us threw caution to the wind, starting to take things out on those around us. Intentional or not, it's a shocking reminder of how fragile our cohesion can be, and a true test of its tensile strength in the face of a global pandemic.

Every time one of these incidents occurs, the topic of maintaining racial harmony and "keeping the peace" is swung around like a baseball bat in cyberspace, before fading into silence once amends are made and apologies given. It's always been a thorny and touchy topic to approach in Singapore – especially when one's own ethnic lenses can unintentionally cloud judgement and blur perspective on such matters. As an ethnic Chinese myself, at some level, I could never even begin to understand how minorities would feel growing up in a country where the majority of folks are of a different race. Then again, I often forget how my own ethnicity has changed my views on multiculturalism. Growing up in a Peranakan household, I was surrounded by a culture so rich in colour and vibrancy, its scintillating nature often bordering on being overwhelming. My childhood memories are full of indulging in rich foods, wearing technicolour *batik* clothes, and hearing my relatives converse in a flood of Baba patois.

As I grew older, I found myself often at a crossroads with my identity: was I Chinese, or not? And if I was Chinese, how *pure* was I? These questions eventually drove me to resent my Chinese roots. For a long time, I felt that I *had* to choose one – be Peranakan, or be Chinese. However, I eventually realised that I could be both, and that I *was* both. A larger epiphany struck me then, that being made up of more than one identity was what it meant to be Singaporean. None of us are 100% Chinese, Malay or Indian – we enjoy each other's foods, we celebrate each other's holidays, and we can even speak a little of each other's mother tongue. I realised that Singapore's multicultural landscape is deeply rooted in the amalgamation of its people – and how the exposure to each other's world fosters a greater understanding.

Even as we embrace this understanding, we can sometimes get "too comfortable" – and that's when we can become unintentionally insensitive.

Fighting a Different Virus of Racial Tensions

Sensitive topics are aplenty in Singapore – sex education and gay rights are just two that come to mind. However, race and religion still stand out as the two that Singaporeans just won't talk about, lest they offend the other race and cause unnecessary tension. But this tension is necessary for us – to understand what we've been doing wrong, what we can do better, and how we can learn from our mistakes, instead of regurgitating the same old values year after year, and reciting them like a mantra when these events occur.

> For a long time, I felt I had to choose one – be Peranakan, or be Chinese... I eventually realised I could be both, and *was* both. A larger epiphany struck me... being made up of more than one identity was what it meant to be Singaporean.

Making mistakes is part of every learning process. So why can't we allow ourselves to make mistakes here and learn from them? The sooner we start, the better.

The times are changing

The annual National Day Rally speech given by the Prime Minister always provides a yardstick for our national progress and standing in the world. For the past few years, the speeches have seldom even checked in on the topic of racial harmony, let alone mooted change. However, PM Lee Hsien Loong's 2021 speech placed the touchy subject front and centre.

For a long time, there has been controversy surrounding the government's stance on nurses wearing the *tudung* (Muslim headscarf). For many Muslim women, it's an indispensable part of their religious identity. When the announcement came allowing nurses to wear the *tudung*, many Singaporeans were in support of the amendment, myself included.

2021 has been a terrible year for racial relations. We've had so many public displays of racially fuelled hatred and angst that I've lost count. Sooner or later, the government had to step in to patch things up and give us respite. It would seem appropriate, then, that the government has made some sweeping changes this year to try and nip racial discrimination in the bud. The *tudung* issue had been widely discussed for many years, behind closed doors. What's truly outstanding now is the government's new approach to dealing with racial issues.

Heavy-handedness has always been a quality associated with the Singapore government. Be it laws, fines or curtailing press freedom, the methods of dealing with undesirable behaviour have always been severe. With the new Maintenance of Racial Harmony Act, the government hopes to incorporate "softer and gentler touches" that focus on persuasion and rehabilitation. This is a crucial change. Helping offenders understand why such behaviour is frowned upon is key in ensuring that such actions are not repeated. Imposing punishment upon racists and xenophobes and hoping that the punishment itself serves as the lesson can breed an even deeper discontent and hatred, which could fester into a permanent hatred for other races.

Changing attitudes, instead of just forcing and enforcing hardline laws, is the new way forward in dealing with racial issues. Helping people understand why they're wrong has more value, instead of just insisting that they are wrong outright. But this can only work if Singaporeans are receptive to change, and

Fighting a Different Virus of Racial Tensions

if they are willing to have the difficult, but necessary, discussions about race.

The youngest contributor to this book, 19-year-old **Billy Steven Tay** is a scriptwriter, journalist and TV producer in Singapore. He has written, and photographed for, articles about Baba and Nyonya culture for The Peranakan Association, and produced current affairs content for national broadcaster Channel NewsAsia's digital arm, *CNA Insider*. On the personal side, he is an avid record collector and music writer, writing about the history of music, while unearthing, preserving and documenting rare and lost music artefacts from all over the world.

Dialogue, Differences and Empathy: How Theatre Can Facilitate Deeper Engagement with Multiculturalism

AUDREY WONG

The conventional narrative of Singapore during the early years of independence centres on how our founding fathers chose the path of political pragmatism and a focus on economic goals, and paid little attention to arts and culture. However, in their mission to construct a nation, our founding leaders were sensitive to culture as an ideological tool, affirming the importance of each ethnic community's connection to their respective cultural roots. The state attempted to define these cultural roots for the people.

In 1967, then-Deputy Prime Minister Goh Keng Swee spoke about the qualities of a distinctive Singapore play, in a speech at the Victoria Theatre, proposing that it reflect the "realistic life of Singapore and its multi-racial, multi-cultural and multi-religious spirit", and also reflect the qualities of the ideal Singaporean such as patriotism, diligence, and a sense of responsibility. The state

Dialogue, Differences and Empathy

needed a population who would be law-abiding and place nation above self-interest, and thus, cultural values were identified with national values.

As scholars such as Terence Chong have argued, the state has always "harnessed" the arts and culture for national-ideological ends, including projecting a vision of multiracialism rooted in what many scholars have criticised as essentialised CMIO racial categories. The monolithic imagination of cultural identity ignored the actual diverse linguistic, ethnic and cultural landscape of the country.

Artists, on the other hand, thrive on diversity, and seek to express everyday multiculturalism and identity formation as lived and experienced by people at home, at work, in the neighbourhood and other social settings. And that experience of multiculturalism might be one of "everyday dissonance" as described by Mathew Mathews in his introduction to the book *The Singapore Ethnic Mosaic* (2018). Mathews illustrates this with a survey by the Institute of Policy Studies which revealed that while Singaporeans support multicultural values and believe that all races are equal, a belief in racial stereotypes persists.

As artists may produce works that critique official state narratives, there are occasional conflicts between artists and the state. Artistic content on matters of race and religion, or depicting tension between races, is considered sensitive. Such content includes negative portrayals of problems experienced in ethnic communities. A well-known example was Elangovan's 1999 play *Talaq*, about domestic abuse in a Tamil-Muslim marriage, which the authorities did not allow to be performed in English. To many, such actions on the part of the state shut down discussion of social problems and do nothing to solve them. Instead, this takes away the potential for civic and social groups to resolve community problems.

As Singapore's arts scene matures, theatre groups have successfully presented works with nuanced discussions on the complexities of race, religion, and multiculturalism – for example, Alfian Sa'at's 2009 play *Nadirah*, which focused on a young Malay-Muslim university student, her relationship with her non-Muslim boyfriend, and her mother, who is a Muslim convert.

Despite these developments, as many arts organisations rely on grants from the National Arts Council (NAC) and are required to obtain an Arts Licence from the Infocomm Media Development Authority (IMDA) for public performances, they still need to negotiate the terrain between what is and is not permitted. The NAC's grant conditions include a clause which expressly disallows the staging of works that "denigrate or debase a person, group or class of individuals on the basis of race or religion, or serve to create conflict or misunderstanding in our multicultural and multi-religious society".

Notwithstanding these limitations, Singapore theatre has managed to articulate everyday multiculturalism and tackle the cognitive dissonance between the state's idealised vision of multicultural unity and the individual's experience of race, culture, and identity.

Actions on the part of the state shut down discussion of social problems and do nothing to solve them. Instead, this takes away the potential for civic and social groups to resolve community problems.

This essay reflects on the work of two theatre companies, The Necessary Stage and Drama Box, and considers how their works

Dialogue, Differences and Empathy

allow audiences to confront the ambiguities of everyday multiculturalism and the differing perspectives and values of various groups in society.

In a country where official arenas for discussion of sensitive race issues are limited, the theatre stage provides a safe space for Singaporeans to think about, speak about, and develop nuanced interpretations of themselves as multicultural citizens.

Embodiment and empathetic thinking through forum theatre

One of the early successes depicting racial differences in Singapore was The Necessary Stage's *Mixed Blessings*, first staged in 1993. This was a play about an Indian boy who dates a Chinese girl, and the consternation this causes in their families. The work was in the format of forum theatre, where a dramatised dilemma is first portrayed by actors and then replayed with a facilitator inviting the audience to actively propose solutions by briefly taking the role of one of the characters on stage.

Alvin Tan, a founder of The Necessary Stage, recalls a particularly impactful solution proposed in one performance. An audience member chose to take the role of the son during a powerful scene of conflict with the parents, and switched the emotions of the scene by kneeling before the mother and asking for forgiveness. The audience member had tapped into her cultural and emotional awareness to propose a solution that was not based on logical argument against racist attitudes, but was rooted in an appeal to emotions and customary practices – an appeal to the character's love for her child and a deeply ingrained value of filial piety.

Forum theatre proposes that audiences (the public) have

agency and the power to devise solutions to socio-political dilemmas. This happens through a process of dialogue and active participation. Forum theatre was developed by Brazilian theatre practitioner Augusto Boal under a broader concept of Theatre of the Oppressed and was originally intended to empower those on the margins of society. The audience is termed a "spect-actor" and is "consciously performing a responsible act" – that is, the action of taking on a role in the enacted scene proposes that the audience member has agency.

The spect-actor is simultaneously in a world of fiction (on the stage) and in reality, as she brings her life experience into the dramatic situation. Such a process of embodiment allows the spect-actor to be aware of the inter-subjectivity of human relations and their capacity to take action in a world shaped by intersections between the personal, social and political. In *Mixed Blessings*, the audience is invited to reflect on, and experience, how attitudes towards racial difference play out in interpersonal relations.

Drama Box holds the distinction of presenting the longest-running forum theatre piece in Singapore theatre history – the play *Trick or Threat*, which was first presented in 2007 and remains in the company's repertoire. *Trick or Threat* is a response to the post-9/11 global political climate in which even peaceful Singapore worried about acts of terror.

The dramatic dilemma presented in the play involves five Singaporeans of different races trapped in an MRT train carriage because of a bomb threat. One of the passengers is a Malay man whose traditional Muslim garb leads the others to view him with deep suspicion, even though he is not the only Malay man on the train. The other is a young man who is on the train with a Chinese colleague; he believes that his colleague is favoured at work because of racism. Then there is an interracial couple – a young Chinese man and an Indian woman who believes her boyfriend's mother is racist. Against the backdrop of a larger global problem in which Singapore is enmeshed, a number of other interracial tensions in everyday life, such as Chinese privilege and casual racism, are played out.

Trick or Threat covers issues that are both politically and racially sensitive, given the largely unspoken fear that local Malay-Muslim men might have been radicalised into an extreme form of Islam that justifies acts of violence. Indeed, the first staging of the play almost did not happen. Drama Box had intended to present it as an outdoor performance in Woodlands Civic Centre, but the authorities refused their request to do so and insisted it had to be staged indoors. The eventual compromise was a performance under a large tent in the public plaza.

The authorities' fears proved unfounded, and the play continues to be presented, often to students to educate them about racism. Accompanying the performances are resource kits for students and teachers, with activities for continuing the discussion on racist language, understanding, and mindset change. The fact that it is still relevant suggests Singapore still has some way to go before we can transcend existing barriers between ethnic groups.

The 2007 staging of *Trick or Threat* modelled cross-cultural sensitivities in the facilitation of audience participation. A pair of facilitators (one Malay, one Chinese) ensured that everything that was said by the audience was translated into three languages – English, Malay and Chinese – so that all present could understand the proceedings.

A reviewer of this performance observed how, when a young girl in a miniskirt was about to take over the role of the Muslim man in the re-enactment, one facilitator asked the Muslims in the audience if it was all right for the girl to wear the character's *songkok* (cap). Skilled facilitators fluent in cross-cultural dialogic encounters can create a safe space where views presented by the spect-actors are treated with respect and the empathetic intelligence of participants can be elicited.

The 2007 brush with the authorities was not the first time that the state had problems with forum theatre or these two theatre companies. In 1994, the state announced proscriptions on forum theatre and performance art which amounted to a de facto ban on these forms. The NAC would not fund these art forms, and anyone wishing to stage such works had to post a $10,000 security bond, an amount well beyond the means of local arts organisations. These proscriptions happened at the same time that *The Straits Times* published a report about The Necessary Stage's Alvin Tan and Haresh Sharma attending Theatre of the Oppressed workshops in New York and the Marxist roots of Augusto Boal. Despite the proscriptions, Drama Box retained its commitment to forum theatre work, even though it had to seek other sources of funding as NAC withdrew its grant to the company. The conditions on forum theatre and performance art were lifted in the early 2000s.

Drama Box's command of socially engaged theatre practice is well-demonstrated in *The Lesson*, a participatory play first presented in 2015. Here, the company incorporates a workshop-facilitation style within an immersive theatre staging. The play involves non-actors in the presentation of a scenario of a neighbourhood town planning dilemma, where a new MRT station is

Dialogue, Differences and Empathy

to be constructed but in order to make way for it, another facility – such as a halfway house, a columbarium, a wet market or a hospice – has to be demolished.

The audience moves between designated spots, representing each of the spaces under threat, and at each of these stations, the audience – total strangers brought together in a temporary fictive reality – have the opportunity to debate various positions on questions of value, perceptions of social utility and community good. The debates lead to a final vote by all the audience, choosing the top two sites for demolition.

According to the rules set by the play, the final decision will be given over to the authorities if there is no clear majority vote. This caveat has the effect of the spect-actors feeling that they have a stake in the final choice through their participation in the play's imagined scenario. They briefly embody a process of communal debate, decision-making, and the testing of a social commons.

At the heart of Drama Box's work is a process of "call and response", of dialogue and listening to the concerns of the community and incorporating participatory methods where community members co-create with them. Woven into this approach is empathetic listening, or listening with an attitude open to the possibility of having one's mind changed in a way that enables one to take action to improve lives.

Returning to *Trick or Threat*, the possibility of a changed mind rests on an individual becoming aware of assumptions and blind spots in attitudes towards other races. In *The Lesson*, the embodied process of audience participation and voting allows audiences to change their minds after going through debates with fellow participants.

In the company's own words in 2017, socially engaged theatre is "a democratic way of working, hoping to create a kind of social and cultural relationship, where people can be critical, learn to cooperate if their values coalesce, or learn to co-exist and be empathetic if their values differ".

Saying the "unsayable", and mindset change

Both Drama Box and The Necessary Stage privilege dialogue, and recognise that problems are often rooted in differences between value systems, and in how citizens have been socialised. The process of eliciting empathetic critical thinking might involve discomfort and self-scrutiny.

Sometimes, dramatic impact requires theatre to say what is unsayable in most normal social situations. Characters may make explicit statements about racism – for example, the Indian girl in *Trick or Threat* tells her boyfriend about how his mother sprays air freshener in the room because of her "Indian" scent. Such scenes elicit nervous giggles, often an indicator of a thought or emotion hitting home for the audience.

The unsayable is handled with aplomb textually and visually by The Necessary Stage in *Fundamentally Happy* (2007), a two-hander with a Chinese and a Malay actor. The plot revolves around a young man who returns to his childhood home to look up an old neighbour, now a middle-aged Malay woman. During the course of their conversation it is revealed that the woman's now-deceased husband had sexually abused the young man when he was a child.

The question is whether the woman was aware of the abuse, or had somehow been an enabler. The cross-racial conflict played out before the audience by a Chinese man and a Malay woman wearing a *tudung* – to most eyes, a stereotypical middle-aged Malay homemaker – is powerful. The fact that the abuser is Malay and the victim Chinese risks raising the ire of the authorities, who might view it as inflammatory, with the potential to offend the Malay minority.

The play, however, transcends racial stereotypes through the complex and flawed characters with whom the audience can alternately empathise with and feel angry at. Neither character is a "better" person or the "hero". The play compels us to look beyond race, and towards a more universal issue – that abuse can be invisible and happen in apparently ordinary households regardless of race.

> **Through Kuo Pao Kun's concept of Open Culture... we may arrive at a richer understanding of culture and identity that takes into account not only local cultures but also the impact of extra-territorial forces such as capitalism and globalisation.**

An even more explicit call to considering the possibility of mindset change occurs in The Necessary Stage's bold production, __ *Can Change*, which was originally presented in 2010 and returned for a new staging in November 2021.

The production is a triplebill. In the original production, the playlets were *Homosexuals Can Change*, *Marxists Can Change*, and *Singles Can Change*. In 2021, the third playlet was changed to *Indians Can Change*, a deliberate move by the creators to address recent race-provoking incidents. In the playlets, characters make decisions in their lives where they swing in the extreme opposite direction to their original starting point. For instance, the homosexual character decides he "can" change to embrace a heteronormative life and get married. Characters essentially reject the original values they espoused, to embrace a much more conformist way of life.

___ *Can Change* highlights the polarising effect of intransigent opinions and monolithic social norms. According to writer Haresh Sharma and director Alvin Tan, the intention is to challenge the audience to reflect on the assumptions underlying their attitudes and opinions. As their audience is likely to hold liberal or moderate opinions, it can be difficult for them to accept the characters' decisions. Sharma and Tan believe, however, that those on both the left-liberal and right-conservative wings can be equally obdurate, and those in the middle-ground might be reluctant to publicly stand their ground.

At the end of each performance, the creators facilitate a dialogue with the audience. This is a crucial aspect of the production, with the creators presenting a model of a commons where individuals can either resolve differences or let the differences stand. As Sharma noted in a preview article about the 2021 staging, "the responses that our audiences will have are a result of their lived experiences, and it's really all about learning about these other perspectives, and maybe, we can change to allow these other perspectives to exist as well".

The work of The Necessary Stage and Drama Box invites audiences to practise empathetic listening and critical thinking. They do not accept an easy, simplified view of multiracial co-existence, with "tolerance" as a default setting. We may see here the influence of theatre doyen Kuo Pao Kun's concept of Open Culture, which sees the need to go beyond state-defined essentialist race categories towards a deeper exploration where the individual examines his or her relationship to culture in a way that takes into consideration one's lived experiences, history and memories.

In doing so, we may arrive at a richer understanding of culture and identity that takes into account not only local cultures but also the impact of extra-territorial forces such as capitalism and globalisation. Such an approach is arguably more relevant today, with increasing recognition of the intersectional perspective that the individual's identity is shaped by a complex of social, political, historical and other factors beyond race. As civil society activist Constance Singam wrote in 2010:

> Singaporeans have access to multiple identities – race, ethnicity, religion, culture, nationality and class, as well as others ... For instance, I am Singaporean; before that I was British, and then, for a brief period, Malaysian; I was daughter, wife and housewife. I was young once and am no longer young. I am woman, feminist and social activist, teacher, and writer...

Plays like ___ Can Change and *Fundamentally Happy* recognise intersectionality quite explicitly. Specific social, familial and cultural contexts are in character details and it is understood that a character's choices are not based solely on his or her racial identity. In fact, issues of class, income inequality and race were tackled in Drama Box and The Necessary Stage's collaborative production *Underclass* (2018), where a Malay and a Chinese character meet after the latter loses her job and her flat and moves into a rental HDB unit.

A need for deeper conversations

While I have focused on the work of The Necessary Stage and Drama Box, they are not alone in exploring the rich contexts of multicultural Singapore or hidden faultlines in society. Curious about whether multiculturalism and multiracialism are still important to younger theatre artists, I sampled views from a few practitioners through WhatsApp, particularly asking how they felt conversations about multiculturalism and racialism had changed and whether these are factors in their artistic work.

The three who responded identified that the "hegemonic" racial CMIO (Chinese-Malay-Indian-Others) categories are problematic and have led to a narrow understanding of race and culture. They felt that deeper conversations are needed to arrive at an understanding of true diversity in society, and to go beyond the message of tolerance and "surface-level conversation".

Furthermore, one observed that it is not sufficient to simply "know" about cultural diversity; experiencing it is important. Another noted that many in Singapore are still reluctant to be taken out of their comfort zones. All felt that there was a multicultural consciousness in how they worked, whether it is multiracial casting, assembling a diverse creative team, or directly dealing with related themes in what they write and create. One practitioner explicitly noted the issue of "how race and privilege intersects with class". Their responses echo the call for deeper dialogue and understanding of difference seen in the work of The Necessary Stage and Drama Box.

Theatre practitioners in Singapore have challenged monolithic thinking around multiculturalism and cultural-national identity expressed in the state's discourse. Theatre in Singapore has long been a space to articulate and debate social questions, and theatre practitioners have honed their craft to provide safe spaces for such discussions.

Underpinning the theatrical approaches of The Necessary Stage and Drama Box are an understanding of the importance of open dialogue where the individual recognises their own values and assumptions in contact with others; a recognition of difference; the presentation of lived everyday multiculturalism and how individual biographies intersect with social structures including constructs of race; and finally, the possibility that we can, and do, change our minds because of a process of debate and discussion with others.

There is value in such theatre practices, which remind us about the social commons. Here is theatre's most vital contribution – indirectly, and sometimes imperceptibly – to racial harmony.

Audrey Wong is the Programme Leader of the MA Arts and Cultural Leadership course at LASALLE College of the Arts. She was formerly Artistic Co-director of independent arts space The Substation (2000–2009). From 2009 to 2011, she served as a Nominated Member of Parliament for the arts. She previously served as a board member of the Singapore Art Museum and council member of the National Arts Council, and is currently Chair of the board of non-profit theatre company Nine Years Theatre. She writes and does research on arts management and cultural policy issues. She contributed a chapter to *The Routledge Companion to Arts Management* (2019) and recently co-authored a report for UNESCO Bangkok, *Backstage: Managing Creativity and the Arts in Southeast Asia*.

Beneath Society's Hidden Faultlines

POH YONG HAN

What does it mean to be "one united people?" The title of this book points to an aspiration extracted from our National Pledge, which has been repeated countless times and invoked as justification for various national policies. Yet, nobody really knows whom "one united people" encompasses, or even whether "unity" is always desirable. In this essay, I hope to examine some of the ambiguities and ambivalences around this ideal by unpacking the assumptions that inform it.

Defining "people"

First, who constitutes the "people" when we envision unity? Although various national symbols, institutions, and curriculums have been created post-Independence to help socialise residents into a vision of shared unity, new waves of migration both in and out of Singapore complicate national narratives over our shared histories, identities, and communal loyalties. The government has taken steps to integrate new citizens, setting up the National

Integration Council and introducing citizenship ceremonies and grassroots networks to help support them.

While structure creates order and coherence, it is also implicitly exclusionary, and many of our guest workers are left out of these structures altogether. These include Work Permit holders, such as migrant workers and domestic workers who stay in Singapore semi-permanently on temporary visas, as well as other visa-holders such as those on the EP (Employment Pass) and S-Pass (Short-term Employment Pass).

In aspiring to be "one united people", we should ask ourselves who is left out of this vision, and, perhaps more importantly, why. Who do we think is worthy of being incorporated into the national project, and why does the state seek to mend some faultlines even as it stresses others?

Although this volume aims to look at multiracialism, questions of race cannot be so neatly separated from questions of nationality and xenophobia. Discourses around migrant workers in Singapore, who largely hail from South Asian countries like India and Bangladesh, are one such example. During the height of the pandemic in 2020, a forum letter in the main Chinese daily *Lianhe Zaobao* blamed the outbreak of Covid-19 in the dormitories on migrant workers' "dirty habits", such as the practice of eating with their hands. Although the Minister for Home Affairs K. Shanmugam later categorically denounced the letter as racist, he also mentioned how the letter reflected what a considerable number of Singaporeans genuinely felt.

More recently, debates on the India-Singapore Comprehensive Economic Cooperation Agreement (CECA) similarly show how several strands of discourse can be nested within a single topic. Opposition to CECA has been framed in material, racial, and nationalist terms – there are genuine class-based anxieties over access to job opportunities, nativist understandings of Singaporean identity, and plain old racism against the Indian community. It would be short-sighted to think we can continue operating a bifurcated policy and not expect there to be spillovers in the discourses surrounding race, class and citizenship.

Other lines of disunity?

What might we learn from reflecting on the shifting patterns of dis/unity and the fluid boundaries around identity-making itself?

Singapore has always been a cosmopolitan hub of different people of different nationalities and ethnic origins. Yet, although various historical contingencies have shaped the Singapore government's view that race and religion are the primary social faultlines to pay attention to, a deeper look into our histories suggests that lines of dis/unity were not always inter-racial.

> **It would be short-sighted to think we can continue operating a bifurcated policy and not expect there to be spillovers in the discourses surrounding race, class and citizenship... we should pay attention when "race" is a scapegoat for other factors at play.**

Just over a hundred years ago, the most significant racial riots were intra-, rather than inter-racial; these include the 1851 Anti-Catholic riots between the Catholic and non-Catholic Teochew Chinese, and the 1854 Hokkien-Teochew riots between the two dialect clans' merchant communities.

Similarly, despite sociologists' predictions of co-ethnic solidarity, Sinophobia continues to rear its ugly head in Singapore – observed by various researchers to have been committed by "Singaporean Chinese" against "China Chinese". Clearly, we cannot focus solely or even primarily on race, without situating racial faultlines against a wider context of class, nationality, religion, and gender, to name a few.

These suggest that the way that in- and out-group distinctions have been maintained, and the faultlines that erupt from these distinctions, are not necessarily always racial, but entirely dependent on the wider social and political contexts in which group identities are made salient.

By assuming "race" to be the primary faultline, and by reifying race through various state apparatuses such as the Ethnic Integration Policy and the Group Representation Constituency, the state might inevitably produce the very lines of difference they seek to bridge. Many scholars have written on how "race" itself is an arbitrary marker of difference that has been constituted and reconstituted across space and time, and how many of our assumptions about race have been inherited from the British. Such views give "race" a certain fixity, producing essentialist tropes that become reified through state policy.

Scholars such as Anthony Crothers Milner (of Cambridge University, in the book *The Invention of Politics in Colonial Malaya*), as well as Syed Muhd Khairudin Aljunied (National University of Singapore) and Lian Kwen Fee (Universiti Brunei Darussalam) in journal articles, have looked at the rich cultural and linguistic patchwork of ethnic groups such as the Acehnese, Mandaling and Banjarese who became Malayanised as they adopted Malay as their lingua franca and intermarried with the Malays, suggesting that "Malay-ness" itself was a category subject to redefinition.

Similarly, Abbas Khan (National University of Singapore), in the book *Beyond Bicentennial Perspectives on Malays*, has studied how the Pakistani diaspora became acculturated into Singapore's Malay society, with Singaporeans of Pakistani descent later intermarrying with Malay and Javanese peoples and assimilating into local Malay communities. Hybridisation and transculturation also emerge through intermarriages, giving rise to distinctive communities like the Peranakans.

Despite racial fluidity, the fixity which state apparatuses such as censuses lend to race may ironically amplify racial faultlines when we continue to use Orientalist and culturally deterministic views on race to inform present-day policies. Former Prime Minister Lee Kuan Yew himself believed in racial eugenics, attributing comparative social outcomes in income and education to "a different gene pool" that the Malay community possessed.

Today, policymakers continue to see poverty in the Malay community as a cultural issue, rather than a structural one, as observed in books such as *The Singapore Dilemma: The Political and Educational Marginality of the Malay Community* by Lily Zubaidah Rahim.

Although there are clear historical reasons why the state is wary of race as a faultline, not least given the reasons for Singapore being kicked out of the Malaysian federation, it would also be a mistake to view everything through the lens of race when other underlying faultlines might animate signs of disunity. Justin Gest, a George Mason University anthropologist who has studied white working-class communities in London and Ohio, argues that what appears to be support for racist far-right white nationalist communities in the UK and US are in fact genuine expressions of helplessness and feelings of injustice.

Communities feel like politicians have side-stepped their concerns by prioritising the concerns of immigrants and ethnic minorities and feel unfairly blamed for racial inequalities when they do not feel like their lives have materially benefited from the colour of their skin. How can we reject racist views and still acknowledge their underlying grievances?

In Singapore's context, discussions over whether "Chinese privilege" exists have sparked a flurry of debate, including in the journal *Asian Ethnicity* between Humairah Zainal and Walid Jumblatt Abdullah, and Daniel Goh and Terence Chong. What might be interesting would be to look at how different segments of the Chinese community respond to these debates. For example, who tend to be proponents of "Chinese privilege", or find these terms resonant? Do they tend to be English-educated elites who have studied overseas? What do the Chinese working class think about this topic, particularly those who are Chinese-educated? Different sets of lived experiences, language spheres, and contact with ideas and people, will naturally produce different kinds of norms and expectations.

Thus, we should pay attention when "race" is a scapegoat for other factors at play. For instance, it is possible to argue that the riots mentioned earlier were not about conflict between dialect groups at all, but material conflict between different groups of merchants who happened to be organised by kinship clans, where the Teochew were resentful of the Hokkiens' economic dominance in the lucrative revenue farms tied to gambier and pepper plantations. Similarly, "race" becomes all the more potent as a faultline when it coincides with class, for the lack of cross-cutting cleavages can further segment society and reduce the bridges necessary to pull different social spheres together.

Flipping unity on its head – when disunity might be powerful

Although unity is often celebrated as the ideal to which a society should aspire, our desire for unity may sometimes paradoxically stifle opportunities for real unity. Too much unity is not a good thing, for it could give rise to an ugly brand of Singaporean nationalism that is nativist and exclusive.

Worse, an excessive focus on "unity" might cause us to be averse to conflict, choosing to shut down uncomfortable conversations or managing them through tightly controlled state-affiliated structures. Yet, the possibilities of channelling "disunity" into highly sanitised forms of expression are increasingly limited, given how the accessibility of social media empowers people into providing honest and anarchic expressions of disunity.

The desire to regulate "appropriate" forms of racial grievances can sometimes backfire and exacerbate conflict, such the Ministry of Home Affairs' decision to give artist-activists PreetIpls and Subhas Nair a stern warning in response to their satirical music video on the use of "brownface" in an advertisement featuring a portrayal of different races by one actor.

With new forms of technology and greater avenues for community organising, the state is less able to maintain a monopoly on legitimate avenues and forms of expression. Likewise, instead of seeking to double-down on control, perhaps it should learn how to be comfortable with more playful, satirical, and even provocative, forms of disunity.

After all, lines of acceptability are constantly negotiated collectively, and shift depending on the cultural moment and cannot be determined solely by the state. In an era in which the Internet is a powerful disruptor, the state's tendency to rely on top-down management of racial groups through affiliated institutes and appointed spokespersons for communities may no longer be tenable.

> **An overt focus on state-sponsored unity may also weaken communities' "muscles" in engaging in organic forms of discussions around race.**

Further, an overt focus on state-sponsored unity may also weaken communities' "muscles" in engaging in organic forms of discussions around race. According to research commissioned in 2021 by national broadcaster Channel NewsAsia (CNA) and the Institute of Policy Studies, two in three people said that talking about race creates tensions, suggesting that we have not developed confidence in our abilities to have nuanced and open-minded conversations about race with each other.

Signs of disunity – whether in terms of social media conflicts, or more violent ones such as riots and protests – give important signals as to the underlying faultlines that need to be addressed. Instead of channelling resources into creating structures that would control, regulate, and manage expressions of disunity, perhaps it is more productive instead to explore when and why certain patterns of disunity emerge. How are boundary lines being drawn, and why do some grievances remain unheard?

For one, we must be careful not to mistake outward expressions of unity for genuine unity. Currently, our harmony is finely calibrated through various state laws like the Maintenance of Religious Harmony Act and the proposed Maintenance of Racial Harmony Act. The question is whether we can still sustain such unity in the absence of such infrastructure. After all, laws only go so far – although recent steps to introduce legislation that address racist incidents such as rental racism are laudable, on-the-ground attitudes take far longer to shift.

For another, instead of dismissing expressions of grievances, the state should double down on efforts to identify if certain policies such as the Special Assistance Plan programme and the Singapore Armed Force's personnel policies contribute to systemic racism. Beyond anecdotal evidence, there is a need for greater clarity on how structural policies impact races' ability to achieve economic and social success, which can only come about with greater data transparency.

Perhaps, even as we strive towards "one united people" as an aspiration, we should also realise how impossible this goal is. No society can ever become truly "united" because societies are not static. As an aspirational "global hub" in a wider node of complex flows of people, ideas, and objects, it is only natural that our social landscape will constantly shift, making complete unity unrealistic.

Already, we see how vocabularies surrounding race in the Anglosphere influence local discourse in Singapore, for better or for worse. We in Singapore are not an island unto ourselves, and we find ourselves constantly pulled in multiple directions. As such, racial discourses and movements cannot be examined without looking at the broader and regional and geo-political contexts we are living in.

As Malaysian writer Masturah Alatas has pointed out in the online journal *New Mandala*, it is much more meaningful to understand the dominant position of the Chinese in Singapore vis-à-vis the dominant position of Malays in Malaysia, rather than turn to concepts like "white privilege" which have entirely different historical legacies and social contexts.

The aspiration of "one united people" is admirable, but full of ambiguities and inconsistencies. While we tend to assume racial faultlines to be the most important priority, less attention is paid to how race intersects with class and nationality, amongst other identities. With new migrations, spillovers and slippages are bound to happen.

By paying attention to the historical emergence of faultlines and how in/out-group identities are produced through various state apparatuses and historical contingencies, we can better understand the fluidity of race and avoid being constrained by our own assumptions about its fixities. Finally, we should avoid valorising unity at all costs, for that can lead to a discomfort with disunity and lead us to focus more on preventing disunity than asking how genuine unity can actually be sustained.

Poh Yong Han is a DPhil candidate reading Anthropology at Oxford University. She has an MA in Southeast Asian Studies from the National University of Singapore, and an AB in Anthropology and East Asian Studies from Harvard University.

Unpacking, and Sharing, Ethnic Privilege

DANA LAM

I am a 68-year-old Chinese Singaporean woman. I was born in Singapore, and grew up in Malaysia in the 1950s/60s. I returned to Singapore in 1970 at age 17. I took a job and later went to university here.

The first time I was made aware of the privileged position of being part of the Chinese majority, I was already in my 30s or 40s. You could say this late awakening itself is a privilege. It was the early 1990s. I was a participant in a playwriting workshop. A fellow participant, a much younger man, was reading out from his script. This is the scene from memory:

It is orientation day at a local university. We see the protagonist, a young Indian man, hurrying past the main gates up the driveway towards the administrative buildings. As he nears the cohort of students milling around the buildings ahead of him, his strides slow down. Something happens to the bounce in his step. He notices the pockets of ethnic Chinese all around. He directs his feet towards a group, he notices how the students in the group close the circle a little, turn their backs a little. He hears their prattling in Mandarin. He hesitates; decides on approaching another group. The encounter there is similar.

It is close to 30 years since I heard Haresh Sharma read his work-in-progress. Something about the scene never left me. I was struck by the familiarity of the setting. Groups of ethnic Chinese interacting among ourselves in cosy circles at social spaces, at work, on campus – this was my everyday reality, too. Only the ramifications of our closed social habits on other ethnic individuals were new to me. I was oblivious as any in the privileged majority to the rights of feelings of others not of the same group. In this case, the extent of exclusion experienced by Singaporeans in the ethnic minorities. On a day-to-day basis.

I cannot remember the rest of the script in any great detail. But I remember the shock of it. When he was done reading, I turned to him. "Is this really how you feel?" I asked.

Haresh Sharma is now a celebrated playwright with over a hundred plays to his name. The scene as he described it three decades ago remains quotidian today. I dare say we have all witnessed some version of it. Friends tell me it is hard not to feel left out when the majority Mandarin speakers simply ignore their presence in a group. And this can occur among colleagues in the workplace, in social gatherings among adults. It boggles the mind that, for all the earnest nation-building of the past five decades, including a National Courtesy Campaign (1979), and a Singapore Kindness Movement (1997), we are still backward in civility.

"But, why are *they* so angry?"

But, why are *they* so angry? I have asked the very same question.

Don't we all veer towards groups that are like ourselves? Don't people of minority ethnicities, too, display the same tendency to flock together? Don't we all find comfort in the familiar?

What about the other questions? What about: If we are truly the multiracial society we celebrate, why are we not more familiar, not more comfortable, with each other? Why do we have Deepavali in Little India, Chinese New Year in Chinatown, Christmas on Orchard Road? Why does Channel 8 look like we are a world inhabited by Chinese people, save the occasional comic character of another ethnicity? Why, after more than a hundred years living together, do we have difficulties calling each other's names? Why do some habits still seem odd, some complexions, languages, stereotyped, made fun of. Why do some families have to prep their young school-going children for casual racism – conscious or otherwise – outside of their home? Why is the place of their birth not safer, not more inclusive of them?

Why are *they* so angry? There is that old adage, if the cut is not on you, you don't feel the pain.

In the space of a few months in 2021, we in Singapore were treated to a spectacular, reckless display of the ignorance and arrogance building up among the majority ethnic group. In May, a

Unpacking, and Sharing, Ethnic Privilege

Chinese man attacked an Indian woman in the street for purportedly not wearing her mask properly. In June, a Chinese polytechnic lecturer accosted a mixed-ethnic couple in the street and berated the man for seducing the woman of another ethnicity. Muslim students of the lecturer later revealed that he had targeted them with Islamophobic remarks with regularity. In August, Chinese netizens attacked a national athlete and his family featured on a National Day banner for his Indian ethnicity.

The Prime Minister, in his National Day address a few weeks later, missed the opportunity to reset the temper building in the people. His address in Mandarin was placating, citing the adoption of English as the official lingua franca as a concession by Chinese Singaporeans for the greater good. He said the use of English disadvantaged Mandarin and dialect speakers, which goes to show there is no Chinese privilege in Singapore. What I, and many I know, wanted to hear from the PM was a clear statement of zero tolerance for racism in a multiracial Singapore; and that the arrogance exhibited by certain segments of the ethnic majority is preposterous and must be curbed.

The incidents in May–August 2021 are glaring examples – warning signs, surely – of how casual racism might get out of hand. No law against racism can cover all the terrain. Calling somebody, a subordinate say, "Eh, Melayu!", a co-worker, "*the* Indian" may be convenient, and even amusing, if you are not at the receiving end. If you think it is just harmless ribbing. Think again. What is needed is self-awareness and proper respect for the dignity of others and ourselves.

In July 2019, a police report was made against artist Preetipls and rapper Subhas Nair for profanities targeted at the Chinese majority. The brother-sister team had uploaded a rap video in response to an E-pay advertisement. The ad featured a Chinese celebrity well-known for his comedic turns, in disguises including two "brownface" ones. The duo were not the only ones to object to the advertisement for stereotyping ethnic minorities. The people responsible for the advertisement apologised. So did Preetipls and Subhas. They were subsequently issued a 24-month conditional warning for their transgressions.

> **Today, we have traded the higher functions of discernment, compassion, and tolerance, for the authoritarianism of policing the other.**

The incident was a learning moment for me. I see now how easy it is to be blindsided by an overriding commercial bias. With the stereotyping, the Chinese celebrity is here functioning like the typically attractive female model in, say, car advertisements, as click-bait. The same sloppy thinking applies.

I remember a different time when men traded machismo and racial slurs like they were secret codes of brotherhood. "Eh Tamby, you goondu!" "Eh babi, goondu your sister lah!" It can be volatile, especially when it involves womenfolk in the family. One takes it just that bit too far and the ribbing torches; ignites an explosion. But, another thing can happen. Quite often, one is quick to recognise the signs – a jowl tensing, a red ear – and moves to diffuse the situation. "Eh, brudder, we brudder!" delivered with a rough-and-tumble rugby hold and an incident is averted.

Those were more rugged times. And I am not advocating such behaviour. But here are individuals with the will, and the skills however rudimentary, to negotiate each other's limits. And take responsibility for their actions.

Today, we call the police on the other. We have traded the higher functions of discernment, compassion, and tolerance, for the authoritarianism of policing the other.

How did we come to this?

- I put it down to an over-zealous nation-building agenda. The schizophrenia. The hysteria. The silos created, inadvertently or otherwise. The mixed signals from policymakers.
- Preponderant middle-class aspirations, market forces, competition, and the exclusionary gaze they produce – these drive consumption and the production of the likes of that brownface advertisement. In turn, this feeds further consumption of more-of-the-same and excludes difference. For example, minority faces are hardly, if ever, seen in product advertisements. Such discrepancies have wrought deep-rooted anxieties in people. And the anxieties manifest in episodes of distrust and intolerance for the unfamiliar. For each other. *Us* and *them*.
- The inherent divisiveness of our language policies has been called out many times by academic commentators and civic observers. The same agenda that privileged English language users from the 1970s and closed Nanyang University in 1980, created SAP (Special Assistance Plan) schools that cater to academically strong students who excel in both English and Chinese.

- An artificially wrought mother tongue is swollen in place where there used to be a polyphonous vernacular. A mother tongue that in reality is often nobody's mother tongue. More unfortunate is the perceived privileging of Chinese language, Chinese values and traditions, vested in this and SAP schools.
- The same agenda that conflates Asian values with Chinese values (Confucianism) and regularly broadcasts its desirability must surely recognise the special status it confers on the majority ethnic group. And the alienation, distaste, and unease this causes ethnic minority citizens.
- Not to mention policymakers' repeated insistence that Singaporeans are "not ready" for a Prime Minister from the minority races.

Malay and Indian SAP schools, and other proposals
We need to reset. We need to move out of our respective silos, and learn afresh to listen, to relate, to negotiate, to trust. Some things to rethink:

- SAP schools should be accessible to all races. A Chinese school for Chinese people is irrelevant in a multiracial country. If, indeed, we are invested in racial harmony, what better way than to have the different races studying each other's culture together?

    As it is, generations of Chinese Singaporeans are spending their formative years with absolutely no contact with other races. And this includes some teachers who, after a career in SAP schools, cannot tell the difference between Indian, Indian Muslim, or Malay names. They have no clue as to others' language, habits, and nature, and are more likely to interact based on stereotypes and misrepresentations. They have no skills and sensitivities with which to read and defuse situations. And, this works both ways.

If, as has been argued, knowing and speaking Chinese is a matter of economic and political survival, then all the more, we should afford the opportunity to all the races living here.

Going by its own logic, it makes sense to introduce SAP schools for Malay and Indian languages too. Proficiency in these other languages and their cultures would surely serve the objectives of diplomacy and economic political survival in the region. Besides enriching future generations with the rewards of a good multicultural education.

- Chinese privilege. Instead of categorically stating that there is no such thing, why not look at where the idea came from? Look at where Chinese and Chinese-ness may have been disproportionately promoted. Where policymakers conflate Asian values with Chinese values. Where by bilingualism we have meant proficiency in English and Mandarin exclusively. Why? How can this change?

All is not lost.

A friend from a minority race I had a conversation with recently is hopeful. He likens the prospects for racial equality to the progress of gender equality. For example, nobody today questions a girl's right to go to school. Or a woman's right to run, or own, a business. He thinks the time will come for us to truly live as equals among the different ethnic groups.

But gender equality has had a very long headstart.

To ameliorate current rifts among ethnic groups, and speed up the healing, we need concerted efforts to raise awareness of racial stereotypes and biases, just as we did for gender equality. We need programmes in the school curriculum and across the board for policymakers, educators, frontline workers, to develop skill-sets to recognise stereotypes, biases and racism in ourselves. We need the will to be hard and honest with ourselves, to recognise our own complicity with the problem, especially if we are from the group that has the bigger share of reach and power. Only then can we find new ways to mend, to interact, to bond, and to truly be with each other as a multiracial society.

For now, it is in the milieu of civil society activists and in the arts that I find company with other ethnicities. At AWARE (Association of Women for Action & Research), I have found willing mentors and lasting friendships from among the multi-ethnic membership. For this, I am grateful.

But for the future, for the sake of our children and our children's children, we must be allowed to talk, to voice our disagreements, our hurt, and to listen deeply without judgement. And not be persecuted. We must endeavour to see each other, hear each other, to truly be comfortable in each other's company.

Dana Lam is an artist-writer and a former President of AWARE (Association of Women for Action & Research).

19

Ageing Well Together: Quiet Social Transformation, with Help from Racial Harmony

Insights from 35 Years of Research on Ageing and Mental Health

KUA EE HEOK

Research on the epidemiology of mental disorders is not just about identifying cases, but also exploring social determinants. In 1986, the Department of Psychological Medicine of the National University of Singapore (NUS) was invited to join the World Health Organization (WHO) team for a global study of dementia. In the ensuing 35 years, the NUS team conducted seven studies on ageing and mental health. The data is massive, culled from the captivating life stories of the several thousand seniors of diverse ethnicities and cultures who were interviewed. What emerges is a picture of how a common purpose – ageing well together – is part of the total living environment that needs racial harmony as one necessary condition.

As we analyse the findings, it is amazing to observe this quiet social transformation in Singapore. In the last five years, there is a carefully planned Age Well Everyday (AWE) programme in the community, run by volunteers to help seniors improve their physical and mental health. This programme – which transcends ethnicity, culture and social class – has promoted social connectedness and stirred a sense of empathy, altruism and collective responsibility. It is a small step in the long journey of nation-building but a giant leap for communal achievement and pride.

What we learned from seven studies in the community
The first study on dementia in Singapore, one of the sites of the WHO global study, was in 1986. The catchment area was at Chinatown, and the NUS team interviewed 612 seniors aged 65 and above. They were all Chinese and predominantly Cantonese and Hokkien. Under British colonial rule, the island was sectored according to ethnicities, and even within Chinatown according to dialect groups. My grandfather came to Singapore circa 1896 and was advised to bunk in with friends in the Teochew enclave around Carpenter Street, Philip Street and Teochew Street. However, in those days, there was very little interaction among people of different ethnicities. Elements of that colonial legacy remain in places like Chinatown even today.

The second study on dementia was in 1990 at the Eunos district, which has a predominantly Malay population. The sample was small – only 149 Malay seniors aged 65 and above. They lived with their families, and we noticed that there was good social support from other relatives and friends who were mostly Malay, living in the neighbourhood of their housing estate.

The third study in 1995 was done in collaboration with the Singapore Action Group of Elders, and this NGO's research base, the Centre for the Study of Ageing, was at Toa Payoh district. We had a larger sample of 2,770 seniors aged 60 and above. About 95% of the cohort were Chinese and only 5% Indian or Malay. We observed that there was not much interaction among the three ethnic groups, and even among the Chinese seniors who mostly felt lonely and isolated.

The fourth study at Jurong in 2012 was the first study on dementia prevention in Asia. A cohort of 1,000 seniors aged 60 and above – 93% Chinese and 7% Malay or Indian – was assessed at our research base, the Training and Research Academy (TaRA) located at Jurong Point Shopping Mall. The Jurong Ageing Study (JAS) was a project to ascertain whether psycho-social intervention through group activities could prevent or delay the onset of dementia. The interventional activities included health education, art therapy, tai-chi exercise, mindfulness practice, gardening and music-reminiscence.

This programme in the community, run by volunteers to help seniors improve their physical and mental health – which transcends ethnicity, culture and social class – has promoted social connectedness and stirred a sense of empathy, altruism and collective responsibility. It is a small step in the long journey of nation-building but a giant leap for communal achievement and pride.

During the research, we noted that the activities had stirred a sense of social connectedness and the seniors began to befriend and take care of each other. For example, the able-bodied seniors would assist their older friends during meals and they began to meet socially at their housing estates.

With the success of the Jurong study, we launched an ambitious fifth project called the Age Well Everyday (AWE) programme in 2015. The concept here exemplified the ecology of resilience – a community helping to enhance the resilience of seniors. The tagline of the AWE programme is: "Preventive medicine in the community by the community for the community". It is a structured and evidence-based programme with measurable outcomes. The AWE programme includes health education, mindful awareness practice, exercise, music-reminiscence, art activities and gardening.

We collaborate with the People's Association, and there are now eight community centres with about 2,500 seniors comprising 92% Chinese and 8% Malays or Indians. Volunteers are trained to organise the programme, and we notice that there is good cooperation among seniors from the different ethnic groups. For example, in Queenstown, the group is led by an Indian retiree, Mr Gopal Kanapatty, the Eunos group by a retired Chinese woman, Ms Maggie Sim, and the Malay group at Tampines by a retired army serviceman, Mr Abdul Rashid.

The staff and research team of the NUS Mind Science Centre, who spearhead this programme, meet all the volunteers four times a year to discuss new ideas and allow them to share their experiences of running the AWE programme in their community centres. The feedback sessions provide us with valuable information on the sensitivities of different ethnic groups, and will enable us to improve on the activities when we roll out the programme in other community centres in future.

In 2016, we started a sixth study at the Hannah Day Centre at Toh Yi Drive in Bukit Timah. The aim of this project is to explore the idea of ageing-in-place, which is now in the national conversation, and refers to the ability to live in one's own home and community safely, independently and comfortably, regardless of age, income, or ability level. The Community Health and Intergenerational (CHI) study is led by a psychiatrist, Professor Rathi Mahendran, and has a cohort of 990 seniors. The focus is on the theme of ageing-in-place – exploring family interaction to enhance bonding and community support from volunteerism.

This research is still in progress, with the family study headed by a statistician, Professor Wilson Tam, and the volunteerism by a psychiatrist, Professor Johnson Fam. There is also a project by a nurse, Professor Shefaly Shorey, to train seniors to provide counselling in a study called "Where There Is No Psychiatrist". Social engagement and support are important factors that contribute to multiple health outcomes, and also, indirectly, to racial harmony – family support being a critical component of the social network.

The current national vision of making Singapore "a city in nature" aims to restore nature into the urban fabric, which includes retrofitting concrete canals with grass banks just like natural rivers. This has spurred much more interest in the green environment. Green urbanism is a vital aspect of a resilient and liveable city. The seventh project was the Nature and Mindful Awareness Study (NaMAS) – a small pilot study with 25 seniors of middle-class background and mean age of 68.5 years. They walked mindfully through the rainforest of the Singapore Botanic

Gardens for 10 consecutive Saturdays from September to November 2019, and were assessed qualitatively on physical, mental and social health.

At the end of this study, we observed that they began to know each other better and there was a sense of empathy and care. In this time of the Covid-19 pandemic, they help each other and assist older friends to purchase masks, groceries or medicines.

Regardless of age: How community support can help with ageing well

There will always be a Chinatown, Malay Village and Little India in Singapore. Each with their unique heritage adds to the beauty of the cultural tapestry of this cosmopolitan island. The British colonial divide-and-rule strategy for race relations recognised this reality of ancestral identity and cultural belonging in separating the main ethnic groups. With this inherited model, it was a formidable challenge after secession from Malaysia on 9 August 1965 for Singapore to try and build a new nation comprising immigrants of such vast diversity.

Even today, it would be impossible to attempt to blend the cultures into one melting pot with everything mixed together, because each ethnic group is proud of its own rich and distinctive ancient heritage. Nation-building requires much more effort to go beyond such "conceptual segregation".

Insights from studies on ageing well can perhaps add important perspectives to the current reflections on racial harmony. Many seniors, whether in private or public housing estates, will encounter mental health problems later in life. In the Toa Payoh study, the mostly Chinese seniors felt lonely and socially isolated, leading to a higher prevalence of depression. Because of social changes in the Singapore family such as lower rates of marriage and childbirth, more seniors will be living alone in future. The Eunos study showed that most of the seniors lived with their families and there were other relatives and friends in the neighbourhood who provided social support – thus, the rate of depression was low among these mostly Malay seniors. The family and social support network in Eunos has engendered ideas for the Community Health and Intergenerational study team in the research on ageing-in-place.

For the future, there must be a paradigm shift in planning for the well-being and care of seniors in Singapore, with some earlier presumptions needing to be refreshed. The seven studies have indicated that most seniors in the age group 65–79 years are not frail, depressed or demented. In the Jurong Ageing Study, about 20% were still working full-time or part-time, and in the Age Well Everyday (AWE) programme many volunteers are the "new-old" aged 65–79 years. The AWE programme promotes social connectedness and builds trusting relationships among the different ethnic groups to strengthen group cohesiveness. There is bonding among the groups and the seniors become more supportive of each other as they make new friends in the neighbourhood. This fosters a sense of belonging, acceptance, respect and communal pride as they learn from friends of different ethnicities and cultures.

The findings of the Jurong Ageing Study five-year follow-up were presented at the 2020 World Congress of Psychiatry. In the original cohort of 1,000 seniors, the prevalence of depression was 7.33%, anxiety 1.58% and dementia 1.88%. On reassessment of the cohort after five years, the prevalence of depression was 4.47%, anxiety 0.96% and dementia 2.87%. The rates for depression and anxiety had improved although the rate for dementia increased slightly. The results show that psycho-social activities are effective and that social connectedness is a crucial factor with the active collaboration of seniors of all ethnic groups. The success of this study is a feather in the cap of all the seniors in the research.

The AWE programme is a non-drug approach with community support, and the psycho-social activities are inexpensive. If it can be implemented in more communities, the cost savings in future years will be enormous for families and the health authorities – thus, this kind of "preventive medicine" should be emphasised in the national health plan. Using culturally appropriate and locally relevant activities has contributed to the programme's acceptability among the seniors. It must also be emphasised that the success of the AWE programme hinges on volunteerism and financial support from many donors.

The national aspiration of "one united people" should obviously begin early in school. In this same spirit, we are planning other programmes for young people and one example is the introduction of the Nature and Mindful Awareness Study to schoolchildren and university students. Impactful programmes in the

Impactful programmes in the community on mental resilience will also enhance positive perception of mental disorders and help debunk the associated stigmas – this is important as "one united people" must also be inclusive of people with mental health problems.

community on mental resilience will also enhance positive perception of mental disorders and help debunk the associated stigmas – this is important as "one united people" must also be inclusive of people with mental health problems.

The translational relevance of our community research is to introduce the AWE programme to all community centres in Singapore, as part of the national aspiration towards "one united people", regardless of age. The task ahead is to spur an even deeper sense of empathy and altruism in the community with a programme conceived by the people from ground-up and not with a top-down bureaucratic approach. We need to harness the latent energy of many seniors, especially the "new-old" with untapped organisational skills which are pivotal for the success of the community activities. The spirit of *gotong royong* (Malay for "mutual assistance"), or working together to galvanise the community for a common purpose, is a sine qua non.

And just as absolutely necessary will be a consensus on, and a commitment to, an even more mindful fundamental appreciation of racial harmony. Can Singapore succeed in this national endeavour? Only time will tell, but, with a rapidly ageing society, time is not on our side…

Professor Kua Ee Heok (MBBS (Malaya), MD (Singapore), FRCPsych (UK), PBM, BBM) is the Tan Geok Yin Professor in Psychiatry and Neuroscience at the National University of Singapore (NUS), Emeritus Consultant at the National University Hospital, and Consultant Psychiatrist at Mind Care Clinic, Farrer Park Medical Centre. Previously, he was Head of Psychological Medicine at NUS, and CEO and Medical Director at the Institute of Mental Health. A member of the

KUA EE HEOK

WHO team for the global study of dementia, he was a former President of the Pacific Rim College of Psychiatrists. Trained as a doctor at the University of Malaya, Kuala Lumpur, he received postgraduate training in psychiatry at Oxford University and geriatric psychiatry at Harvard University. He has published 310 research papers and 30 books on psychiatry, stress and ageing. He is Editor-in-Chief (with Norman Sartorius) of the seven-volume series, *Mental Health and Illness Worldwide* published by Springer-Nature. His novel, *Listening to Letter From America*, is used in a course on anthropology at Harvard.

Notes Towards a Few Breakthroughs to True Unity

LAURENCE LIEN

When foreigners ask me what I, as a Singaporean, find most unique about Singapore, I often say that it is Singapore's racial and religious harmony. I urge them, for example, to go to Waterloo Street where on one short street they can find a Jewish synagogue opposite a Catholic church, and a Buddhist temple next to a Hindu one. Or I encourage them to visit a typical residential neighbourhood, where they would see a diversity of races accessing, and living in, shared spaces.

However, tolerance does not equate to harmony, and the remarkable lack of racially motivated altercations does not mean that ties are flourishing. As Singapore matures as a society, there are concerns that Singaporeans' commitment to Singapore, and to one another, will wane in the face of more diversity among the population, particularly as we face more turbulence in the economy. Racial and religious cleavages, which are manageable in good times, can become amplified in bad stretches.

LAURENCE LIEN

In this essay, I will provide a quick overview of my observations of how racial and religious relations in Singapore stand today, and then make a few concrete recommendations that we can adopt so that we can evolve our society into one that is even more united and cohesive. I am not qualified to make any definitive conclusions, but hopefully, my perspectives will be useful in providing new insights into a highly complex subject matter.

Is Singapore more united today?

In many aspects, Singapore seems a lot more united racially and religiously today than a few decades ago. When I was growing up, I could not count any person of a different race as a good friend, whereas each of my sons has good friends from a different race. Few of my friends dated or married someone from a different race. Today, about one in five marriages are inter-ethnic, a large increase from the one in 10 just two decades ago.

Over the years, studies like the 2016 Channel NewsAsia-Institute of Policy Studies (CNA-IPS) Survey on Race Relations have found that fewer people stereotype a person based on race, trust in all races has increased, and Singaporeans are in large proportion positive about the level of racial and religious harmony here.

Hence, by any objective criteria, Singapore has done creditably in racial and religious relations. But beyond the topline numbers, there are persistent issues that refuse to go away. For example, in the CNA-IPS survey, nearly 50% of respondents still recognised that racism can be a problem, and are aware that there are substantial portions of Singaporeans who are at least mildly racist.

Notes Towards a Few Breakthroughs to True Unity

It could be that we have addressed some of the easier and more basic challenges, and are left with the more difficult ones, like stubborn stains. It may also be because we have grown complacent, and the world around us is changing in ways that are making racial and religious differences more salient.

Let me highlight three personal observations on race relations, as I try to make sense of the context today.

Why is there more workplace discrimination?

My first observation is the increase in claims of workplace discrimination. A 2019 IPS-One People.sg study revealed an increase in minority groups perceiving workplace discrimination, for instance when applying for jobs. About a third of the Malays and Indians surveyed, for example, often or sometimes felt racially discriminated against while at work.

What is the source of this? Let me posit a few hypotheses. One, the definition of success. In an increasingly achievement-oriented society, we have defined success according to fairly narrow meritocratic dimensions. These dimensions may make it challenging for some ethnic groups, who may embrace a broader definition of success, to "keep up".

Two, the impact of our immigration policies. In maintaining the racial proportions at the aggregate level, we have given employment and residency to Chinese and Indians from countries and cultures different from ours. When the numbers of these foreign employees in a workplace environment reach a critical mass, it may make it even difficult for Singaporeans of the same race, let alone a different race, to fit into the workplace culture. Hence, for example, a Mandarin-speaking worker, as well as a

Mandarin-speaking customer, may have no incentive to learn English when the vast majority of staff can converse easily with him or her. It is easy then for a non-Mandarin speaking Singaporean to feel excluded.

Three, racial biases. Racial stereotypes that simmer below the surface can sometimes boil over when left unattended. We are all familiar with ingrained prejudices about each race that do not need repeating here. At one of my workplaces, we had a Malay intern who introduced us to a graphic design company, run and staffed by Malays, to conceptualise and design our publications. I was hesitant, as they lacked the usual confidence in their pitch, and lowballed their quote. But I gave them a try, and ended up surprised by their high quality, and embarrassed by my own initial preconceptions.

It could be that we have addressed some of the easier and more basic challenges, and are left with the more difficult ones, like stubborn stains. It may also be because we have grown complacent, and the world around us is changing in ways that are making racial and religious differences more salient.

The rise of identity politics in times of stress

My second observation is that, in times of personal and family stress, the negative force of identity politics would tend to surface.

We each have multiple identities. Identity is a social construct that emerges when an individuals and groups interact with one another in society. These identities are formed along the lines of race, gender, religion, socio-economic status, age, and so on. Each identity is, in turn, defined by societal expectations and social norms, even as an individual would try to continually reshape that identity, resulting in a highly dynamic process. Whether a particular identity is salient depends on the context, and whether we are able to find commonality and intersections in other identities that we possess.

In Singapore, the dominant social marker is socio-economic status. During times of great social mobility, and where a rising tide lifts all boats, we are able to adopt mutual cooperation and reciprocal understanding as a main mode for relating to one another. Dealing with racial and religious diversity may then become less relevant.

On the other hand, when wealth and income divides grow, and with heightened competition for jobs and resources, there is a need to ask — as one observer, Professor Katherine Marshall of Georgetown University in the US, has asked, in the book *Faith, Identity, Cohesion* (2020) — whether the success of Singapore's multiculturalism is tethered to its economic success, and, if decoupled from high levels of development and employment, whether the cohesiveness of the country's diversity can persist, or, in fact, erupt into outright conflict.

Is there enough meaningful mixing?
My third observation is that day-to-day inter-ethnic relations are insufficiently deep. We are understandably proud of our ethnically diverse neighbourhoods. However, just living in the same estate does not mean that there is meaningful social mixing. We are all too aware of how often we hear of Singaporeans not knowing any of their direct neighbours. Moreover, racial preconceptions can also frustrate social integration.

A few years ago, I had a team that conducted ethnographic work at an award-winning new Housing & Development Board (HDB) estate that had more than 2,000 units running the gamut from rental flats for lower-income tenants to five-room flats. There were three playgrounds in the estate, and it was revealing how, over time, signs that forbade the playing of football appeared only at the one playground right in front of the five-room block. It seemed that the relatively higher-income residents from that block did not want their kids playing football with the kids from the rental block, who were disproportionately from one race.

Possibilities for tomorrow: Stronger communities, inclusive capitalism, diverse schools
Where can we go from here? Let me suggest a few policies and practices that we can review.

The first area is to build stronger communities. To create a society with a greater sense of togetherness, there are a few ingredients of community development that are critical success factors. These include: one, belief in the strengths of people in the community to initiate positive action, without depending on state help or external resources; two, genuine empowerment, beyond consultation, to grow and share power; three, good community leadership and facilitation, within the community. These ingredients would facilitate more horizontal relationships among residents and build a sense of ownership and engagement.

When I was a Nominated Member of Parliament (NMP), I called for some bold experiments to build social capital, which I will repeat here. I recommend devolving power to elect Residents' Committees in HDB estates to the residents, which following the

Group Representation Constituency (GRC) example, must have the requisite ethnic diversity. Neighbourhoods should be allowed to choose their leaders, just like residents in condominiums choose their management committees. They should be empowered to engage residents to make significant decisions and set rules on how their neighbourhood should evolve and be uniquely organised.

We also need resident leadership programmes to develop competent community facilitators, who are able to catalyse the work of residents and connect them to others to work together. In addition, small seed grants for community projects should be provided for projects initiated, planned and implemented by community members in partnership with the Town Council.

> **Try to narrow the income and wealth gaps, and reduce any spillover social tensions at the workplace. Capitalism needs to be reformed, and companies should foster a meaningful corporate purpose instead. It is not just about making money, but about whether the products are produced in a socially responsible way.**

The second area is to try to narrow the income and wealth gaps, and reduce any spillover social tensions at the workplace. Capitalism needs to be reformed, and companies should foster a meaningful corporate purpose instead. It is not just about making money, but about whether the products are produced in a socially responsible way. Do companies welcome diversity in the workplace? Are they paying a living wage? Are they investing in human capital, job creation and training?

Corporate leaders should act as agents of social change, and should model practices of inclusion. There needs to be diversity training to help employers and employees identify the cultural practices and values that help to bridge, and harness, cultural differences.

In addition, Singaporeans can, and should, pay higher income and wealth taxes. These can be channelled to subsidise essential services, and to insure families against catastrophic episodes. These social safety nets should be available for all Singaporeans, without the excessive conditions that are currently tied to aid.

All these measures can help to form a comprehensive plan to build up the confidence of diverse groups working and living together, so that they feel engaged and confident, and also included and protected. These can go a long way towards every individual enjoying a sense of dignity and fair treatment, so that together, we can focus on commonality and less on differences.

The third area is to start young. We need more ethnically diverse schools and classrooms. All government schools ought to have minority quotas to address under-representation. In addition, I recommend changing our Mother Tongue Language policy to a Bilingual Language policy, with students being able to select a second language that is an official language that is not their "mother tongue". Increasingly, with English being spoken at home as the main language by the majority, "mother tongue" is a misnomer. This would also allow for Special Assistance Plan (SAP) schools, which are more Chinese-oriented, to admit more non-Chinese students.

In schools, inclusive education should be taught, to challenge myths and stop stereotypes and prejudices. This should not be taught as a topic in a classroom subject, but through dialogues in ordinary situations of day-to-day life. Teachers can help create safe spaces for "agenda-less" dialogues, that allow students to break down the walls by sharing perspectives that are not commonly heard, and to develop the desire for mutual respect, understanding and collaboration.

Across schools, we can also encourage youth-led civic action groups. We can recruit students from schools that are demographically different to form common interest groups. They should develop a change agenda, particularly organising around localised issues pertinent to them, like encouraging more recycling or improving traffic safety.

Singapore has done well on racial and religious tolerance and harmony. But tolerance and harmony do not equate to one united people. To make the next quantum leap, we need a series of bold, ambitious and original moves. I have suggested a few, which also intersect with other social impact areas. Leadership and courage are needed, but I am optimistic that the ideals in the National Pledge can be achieved, rather than just aspired to.

Laurence Lien is Chairman of the Asia Philanthropy Circle (APC), a membership-based platform for Asian philanthropists to exchange, learn and collaborate. He is also Chairman of Lien Foundation, a family foundation that has become well-regarded for its forward-thinking approach in education, eldercare and the environment, as well as Chairman of Lien AID, the foundation's humanitarian arm for enabling sustainable access to clean water for Asia's rural poor. He was CEO of the National Volunteer & Philanthropy Centre in Singapore from 2008 to 2014, and Chairman of the Community Foundation of Singapore

LAURENCE LIEN

from 2013 to 2019. Prior to his work in the non-profit sector, he served in the Singapore Government. He holds degrees from Oxford University, the National University of Singapore, and Harvard University's Kennedy School of Government. He was a Nominated Member of Parliament in Singapore from 2012 to 2014.

One United Patois: Singlish and Race in Singapore

COLIN GOH

Singlish – Singapore's vernacular English – is characterised by its liberal mixing of English with terms from the so-called "mother tongues" of the various ethnic groups that make up the country's population.

I don't intend to spend any time analysing whether Singlish is a pidgin, a creole, a patois, an ethnic dialect, or some other category of hybrid language, because that is a complex undertaking which would take me well beyond my remit as an essayist, my primary competency as a humourist, and the patience of my wife. ("You so busy, where got time to go and write this kind of cock?" I can hear her bark, in classical Singlish. "They got pay you by the word, *meh*?")

I nevertheless agreed to contribute this essay, because it is my belief that Singlish is Singapore's only uniquely Singaporean product, and it brings me great joy.

Only one uniquely Singaporean product, *meh*?

It's hard to argue with the country's official stance that this tiny speck of an island really doesn't have any natural resources to speak of, beyond the grit and ingenuity of its people. I mean, our top export are integrated circuits, and I don't think they are grown and harvested from the lush foothills of Tuas.

Singlish is uniquely Singaporean, because it has sprung *organically* from our history. No government committee thought it up or regulates its syntax, and the language is richer precisely because of the absence of official intervention.

But, but, but – I hear some of your splutter – what about our much-celebrated UNESCO world heritage-recognised cuisine?

Let's be honest. Can you think of a purely or uniquely Singaporean dish – one that was clearly invented in Singapore and also not served elsewhere in any similar form? (Say, in a country just north of us, whose citizens habitually dispute the authenticity and provenance of Singaporean culinary creations?)

Also, we continually classify Singapore food along ethnic/racial lines. For example, while we can argue that fish-head curry was invented in Singapore, and loved by all races, we still distinguish between Indian-style, Malay-style or Chinese-style. Meanwhile, we feel compelled to differentiate even a dish like *rojak* – whose name literally means "mixture" in Malay – into whether it is the Indian, Javanese or Chinese version.

We celebrate Singapore food for its buffet of individual artefacts, not really its mixing – whereas we do the opposite with Singlish.

One United Patois: Singlish and Race in Singapore

Cheerfully *chapalang*: The glory of Singlish
The glory of Singlish lies in its unabashed jumbling. A single sentence like "Eh, you go and *kacau* that *goondu*, like damn *song lai dat, meh*?" contains words borrowed from Malay (*kacau* – disturb/provoke), Tamil (*gundu* – thick or fat), the Southern Chinese Hokkien dialect (*song* – satisfying) and, of course, distorted English ("like that").

In standard English, the sentence would go something like: "Did you derive some sort of perverse satisfaction from provoking that idiot?" I am sure most would agree that a certain musicality and charm have been lost in translation.

There is no logic or hierarchy to the expressions we choose to incorporate into Singlish. We use *dabao* (Cantonese) or *bungkus* (Malay) far more than we do "takeaway/takeout". We all use the Malay word *shiok* to express pleasure and the word *gostan* (a contraction of "go astern") to mean "reverse", probably originating from the days of bumboats berthing along the Singapore River. The raising of one's hand in a reverse-slicing motion and the exclamation "*Dey!*" is no longer exclusive to the Tamil population – it is used by a broad cross-section of Singapore society to express irritation and incredulity. Meanwhile, the fastest way to sound Singaporean is to simply double your adjectives – "See the fat-fat guy in the black-black shirt?" – a common practice amongst the Chinese.

The vast majority of Singaporeans understand that Singlish deviates from standard English, and employing it deliberately always carries a tiny illicit thrill. Meanwhile, spotting its use in a foreign country immediately establishes a kind of Proustian connection, based on shared autobiographical memories. (Depending on one's hangups, this could manifest itself as either nostalgia or cultural cringe, but that says more about you than about Singlish itself.)

This libertine mixing of languages in Singlish also lends distinctiveness to our literary arts.

I realise this may trigger some people, but if a Singaporean play doesn't involve at least some Singlish dialogue, what makes the play culturally distinct from, say, Jamaican or Australian or Indonesian or Chinese plays? Absent some Singlish, how does one instantly recognise that a play is set in Singapore, without reading the explanatory notes or critic's exegesis in the programme booklet?

Let me clarify by saying that I am not in any way suggesting that Singlish should serve as a marker of quality or even authenticity. All I am saying is that Singlish functions as an instant signifier of origin and context. Singlish doesn't make a work of literature good, but when you encounter its use, it immediately makes you think: "*Orh, lai dat* must be about Singapore." (Personally, it gives me a thrill to hear it in the theatre, or in the cinema, or in print – like a little impertinent scrawl of graffiti on the fortress walls erected by the more dominant cultures.)

From LC to BBC

Despite its uniqueness, Singlish is not universally celebrated in Singapore.

Language purists see Singlish or any commingling as eroding the sanctity of its constituent tongues, much like those stuffy French folks who would rather people use *"courrier électronique"* instead of "email".

One United Patois: Singlish and Race in Singapore

Singlish users are often perceived as "low-class" (often abbreviated as "LC") or socially inadequate. The Singapore government has said explicitly that it views Singlish as a handicap to the nation's global aspirations.

For example, in his 1999 National Day Rally address, Prime Minister Goh Chok Tong expressed disapproval of the Singlish dialogue in the highly popular TV sitcom *Phua Chu Kang* – arguably the series' most appealing feature.

This outraged me personally. At the time, my wife and I had moved to New York City for graduate school, and Singlish was a way of salving our homesickness. Fearing the erosion of something that brought us so much delight, we set up a satirical website where Singlish was a main feature.

Called TalkingCock.com (a Singlish term descended from the English "cock and bull story" which has actually been debated in Singapore's Parliament on at least three occasions), it regularly racked up four million page views a month, a remarkable feat in the pre-social media age. It was also featured in the BBC, NPR, *The London Times*, and *Time* and *Wired* magazines.

An important part of the site was an online dictionary of Singlish, where we crowdsourced submissions from readers. We compiled and edited hundreds of contributions, and it was later published as *The Coxford Singlish Dictionary* (Angsana Books, 2002), a poke at the Oxford English Dictionary. A bestseller at its launch, it remains in print even after 20 years.

Through the site and the dictionary, we learned how passionate and protective average Singaporeans were about Singlish, all of whom felt that the official crackdown, while perhaps well-intentioned, was wrong-headed.

The anti-Singlish argument, which is still periodically trotted out by the government, is premised on the perceived need for all Singaporeans to speak grammatical English at all times, or risk becoming less attractive to our global clientele. The fear was that any exposure to Singlish would undermine our global competitiveness.

And so, the use of Singlish was restricted on broadcast TV and radio, and even movie trailers, even if not the movie itself. This caused gross perversions in Singapore's media landscape: Singaporeans could watch programmes in French, Italian or any European language on TV, but not our own homegrown tongue. English grammar was butchered any number of ways in American and British shows, but could never be in Singaporean ones.

The "exposure" argument persisted even though it was built on false assumptions. After all, even after decades of importing the majority of our TV and other shows from the USA, we still do not speak with American accents. Meanwhile, after moving to New York City, we witnessed firsthand how so many people just got things done, even with wildly varying accents and commands of English.

Perhaps the worst victim of this campaign was the local

> **Singlish is the one Singaporean product that has grown – organically – from our native soil... you have to admit it is more authentically representative of the multiracial culture of Singapore than any of our culinary offerings, a certain continually expectorating lion-fish hybrid, or any number of National Day Parades.**

One United Patois: Singlish and Race in Singapore

media itself. As Singaporean shows could never contain authentic-sounding dialogue, audiences felt disenfranchised from local programmes. It was telling that when Singlish was inevitably curtailed in the next season of *Phua Chu Kang*, the series declined in popularity and soon ended.

It is telling that over the years, official anti-Singlish efforts have had little impact on stifling the use of Singlish amongst the general populace. In fact, they have either led to pro-Singlish backlashes or inadvertently promoted its delights. Despite periodic harrumphing from officials, Singlish is now ubiquitous in many cultural productions, and advertising, and, increasingly, in the government's own public education efforts, especially in these pandemic partial-lockdown times, closed-off from the rest of the world. This is precisely because the use of Singlish comes across as "authentic".

Chut pattern *liao*

In recent years, however, a new wrinkle has arisen in the Great Singlish Debate. This time, the charge comes not from stodgy conservatives, but rather the "woke" left, who argue that Singlish is not sufficiently representative of minority languages, and its use may make those not born in Singapore feel excluded. In other words, while Singlish used to be pilloried for using too many non-English words, it is now being criticised for not borrowing enough non-Chinese words.

It is true that a lot of Singlish is dominated by Hokkien, and, to a lesser extent, other Chinese terms, followed by Malay, with only a sprinkling of Tamil. And I suppose it is true that like all things, language can be used to exclude.

Is there therefore an argument for regulating or policing Singlish in the interests of racial harmony and representation?

I shudder at the thought of this being tabled for parliamentary debate by some politicians who are insufficiently occupied (a state variously known in Singlish as *gatal*, *eng*, or "itchy backside").

Bochup is best

While I have some sympathy for the underlying sentiment, I fear the unintended consequences of any attempt to regulate what is a living, evolving language. The Singlish terms we use today are already different from those used by our parents and forebears, and no doubt, those used by our kids and grandkids will be different as well. This is the beauty of a living language. After all, do the English in England still greet each other with "Well met, sirrah!" as they did back in Shakespeare's time?

Singlish is also already changing. One interesting phenomenon is how the spelling of dialect terms is now increasingly modelled on *hanyu pinyin* (the romanised form of Mandarin promulgated by mainland China), in contrast to the transliterations used by earlier generations. So "takeaway" is now often written as *dabao* rather than *tar pow*, and *cho bo* (Hokkien for "idle") is rendered as *zho bo*.

> **Enabling everyone to communicate with everyone else – and so, bringing everyone together: This would be Singlish's most vital contribution to racial harmony.**

I do hope that we incorporate more non-Chinese words, but that should be due to popular trends rather than artificial, affirmative insertion. Any demographic changes would also tie up such

One United Patois: Singlish and Race in Singapore

initiatives in knots. Any attempt to mandate what Singlish should, or should not, be would also greatly undermine its libertine – and humorous – spirit, and constrict its nature, possibilities and use.

We know there is such a danger, because there are always unintended consequences of regulation. Even Singapore's trademark bureaucratic efficiency, public cleanliness, law and order, etc., are invariably tainted by various by-products that arise in the process of either design or execution – restriction of civil liberties, stifling of creativity, etc.

Singlish is the one Singaporean product that has grown organically from our native soil, and where the people gleefully use terms borrowed from their neighbours' tongues. You don't have to like it, but you have to admit it is more authentically representative of the multiracial culture of Singapore than any of our culinary offerings, a certain continually expectorating lion-fish hybrid, or any number of National Day Parades. It needs neither regulation nor promotion – let us just marvel as it grows and evolves.

Enabling everyone to communicate with everyone else, and so, bringing everyone together – this would be Singlish's most vital contribution to racial harmony. Here is another unintended consequence – but this time, with deep benefit – whose societal value is so often under-appreciated.

Hence, the best Singlish policy, in my humble opinion, is to heed the words of the *ah beng* building contractor Phua Chu Kang himself: "Don't play-play."

Colin Goh was the first Singaporean to draw a daily comic strip in the newspapers, and the founder of pioneering satirical website

COLIN GOH

TalkingCock.com, which has been debated in Singapore's Parliament, and mentioned in *Wired* magazine, *The Washington Post* and Wiki-Leaks, among others. He's also a lawyer in three jurisdictions; a multiple award-winning filmmaker; the cartoonist behind two *New York Times* bestsellers; and the creator of the children's comic series *Dim Sum Warriors*, which was adapted into a musical in China, acquired by international publishing giant Scholastic, and is now the foundation of a multiplatform bilingual language learning system. He doesn't get enough sleep.

EPILOGUE

The "Geometry of Community"

KOH BUCK SONG

As part of a three-day family holiday cruise to Penang in 2019, on a day's shore excursion, a local Malaysian driver was hired to take us around. Mostly for the benefit of my elderly mother, with her bad knee, we needed his minibus to boost our mobility. Mobility of the socio-economic kind, however, was discussed, as we turned away from the Khoo Kongsi heritage building. Somehow, the conversation turned to how this Chinese-dominated island was managing its racial harmony, long before this book was a glint in its publisher's eye. Our driver, of Indian ethnicity, said: "Everything is fine, so long as people have jobs."

This comment stayed with me as a neat summary of one important strand of the fragility of racial harmony. Everything is fine, so long as everyone believes they have a fair shot at improving their lives. This thread, that holds everything together, has been stress-tested in these pandemic times of loss of income, isolation and disillusionment. Indeed, it can even be said, it is a wonder that the situation in many countries did not get much worse. So far throughout this pandemic, that Singapore has still seen most of the typical serenity that is a hallmark of its society attests to a resilience founded on the essential predisposition towards harmony within its societal DNA.

Landmarks of harmony are quite visible across Singapore's landscape. As Saleemah Ismail highlights, Telok Ayer Street is "Singapore's representative street of religious harmony – home to a temple, a mosque and a church. I believe this is a rare sight not found in many parts of the world."

Beneath the calm, however, the consensus from the essays in this book is that there is more than meets the eye, that latent issues are bubbling just beneath the surface. At one level is Kirpal Singh's admission of a lifetime of abuse suffered as a turbaned Sikh man, "colourfully plagued by fist-fights and verbal abuse arising out of catcalls and racial slurs".

At the other, perhaps least threatening, end of the spectrum, a situation cited by more than one writer is that of a group of Chinese Singaporeans conversing only among themselves in Mandarin in the presence of others. Such exclusion of people of minority ethnicities, as Braema Mathiaparanam notes, happens because "Mandarin has become a lingua franca alongside English, regardless of mixed-race social, work, educational, and recreational environments". This is like a different kind of unwelcome "social distancing" of an earlier era.

Despite the good press Singapore's racial harmony usually receives, for some, the present is actually some distance away from what it could have been. Matilda Gabrielpillai puts it most strongly, recalling her childhood and youth in the late 1950s, '60s and "nation-building" years of the '70s as "the halcyon days of Singapore's multiculturalism, to which we have yet to return".

The "Geometry of Community"

This is because, as she remembers this history, official moves from the 1980s to form a "Chinese cultural elite" have created for Indian, Malay and Eurasian Singaporeans "a story of minority disenfranchisement that has yet to be told".

In similar vein, Dana Lam's rhetorical questions are not easy to respond to, by Singaporeans of any ethnicity: "If we are truly the multiracial society we celebrate, why are we not more familiar, not more comfortable, with each other?... Why, after more than a hundred years living together, do we have difficulties calling each other's names?"

Singaporeans, she argues, have traded the higher cognitive and emotive functions of discernment, compassion, and tolerance, for the "authoritarianism of policing the other", of staying mostly within our ethnic bubbles, calling out perceived racism, when any missteps of racial insensitivity could be smoothed over with more communication and understanding. The contributory factors to this situation, to her, include "an over-zealous nation-building agenda", as well as schizophrenia, hysteria, silo mentalities, and mixed signals from policymakers.

> **Each ethnic community should keep preparing its own "prize dishes" – celebrating distinctive heritage and cultural identities – so as to have even more to bring to the "table", to share at the communal "potlucks" laid out within the shared spaces of society.**

Also advocating peering underneath the veneer of tranquillity, Poh Yong Han cautions that there are hidden faultlines in society, that may create spillovers into other discourses surrounding race, class and citizenship. As a parallel, racist far-right white nationalist movements in the UK and US may in fact be genuine expressions of helplessness and feelings of injustice, she says. This is why it would be wrong to "ironically amplify racial faultlines" by continuing to "use Orientalist and culturally deterministic views on race to inform present-day policies".

Similarly, Nazry Bahrawi cautions that society should remain alert to "covert parallels" – those common threads that might not appear so, at first glance – such as those between the discussions around "blackface" in a place like the US and on "brownface" in Singapore. Being open to seeing what can be learned from the experience of other societies is one way to move towards what he suggests is a better ideal to pursue – that of a "post-racialised society", in which race is not the primary identity marker that dictates how policies and laws are formulated.

There is a need to look beyond any present easy assumptions about the status quo also because, despite the much-discussed incidents of racial insensitivity and racism since the pandemic surfaced, not everyone has had their say yet. Till now, many voices have not been heard much, such as those of the Chinese-speaking Chinese, who see themselves as a linguistic minority, whose voices "seemed to be muffled in our society where English has long been the lingua franca", says Tan Chee Lay. He also notes that factors such as avoidance of race-sensitive discussions by the older generations, and the indifference of the younger generations to this subject due to their relative lack of real-life interaction with people of other races, have contributed to the status quo.

The "Geometry of Community"

Aspects of society in need of a reset

If some issues remain unresolved, certain aspects of society might need a reset.

First, racial harmony should be redefined. Singaporeans might have been lulled into not seeing the reality for what it is, "a pseudo-utopian state where harmony is the order of the day," as Viswa Sadasivan suggests. Society might be underprepared for what the Internet and social media have unleashed – "the truth about us", he argues. Hence, it could be that an excessive emphasis on harmony leads to a false sense of cohesiveness, which could result in complacency.

As Audrey Wong also observes, actions by the state that shut down discussion of social problems may have the side-effect of taking away the potential for civic and social groups to resolve community problems on their own. Such resolution could come about from the safe space of theatre, which can foster reflection that can lead to a richer understanding of culture and identity.

Here is the classic dilemma of censorship of any idea or image in the public domain – deciding on the line between offence and harm. Actual risk of harm – such as someone inciting others to physically attack people of another race – should, of course, be curbed. But some level of offence – say, from something said on a YouTube video – might need to be tolerated, even welcomed, as part of the process towards deeper understanding and, hence, a more genuine and enduring harmony.

Second, some official policies should be reviewed. One of them is the whole CMIO (Chinese-Malay-Indian-Others) model of racial categorisation, essentially a legacy of "ethnic taxonomy" inherited from the days of British empire. As Margaret Thomas, who is of Caucasian-Chinese parentage, argues, it is not race but nationality that gives her her identity. "By sticking these CMIO labels on ourselves, are we making it easier or harder for people to accept someone of a different race, to understand each other better, and to get on better?"

Third, the way society is structured may need some adjustment. The gap between the haves and have-nots is the real issue underlying what appears to be a rise in racist sentiment, says Joyce Lim. To truly live a future in which Singaporeans are one united people might take a kind of capitalism that is consciously more inclusive – "a socially responsible economic and political philosophy that requires reinvention at the highest level".

Similarly, to narrow the income and wealth gaps, and reduce any spillover social tensions at the workplace that might affect racial harmony, Laurence Lien advocates that companies should foster a more meaningful corporate purpose: "It is not just about making money, but about whether the products are produced in a socially responsible way".

Managing life's "Venn diagrams" and society's "potlucks"

So, what behavioural changes might help, on the way forward on this journey of racial harmony?

First, to enhance racial harmony, getting to know each other better is, to put it simply, a great way to start. Kannan Chandran's overall suggestion is for society to speak less of differences, and to spend equal, if not more, time talking about the similarities that Singaporeans share, when all it takes is to have "an open mind and a willingness to find common ground". Empathy is the ultimate

The "Geometry of Community"

goal, and here, schooling in the humanities and the arts – which trains the mind and heart to "walk a mile in someone else's shoes" – is probably the best preparation in youth.

To showcase similarities, speaking a shared lingo is always an asset. And, along the way, a bit of humour surely helps. As Colin Goh notes, Singlish is the one uniquely Singaporean product that is authentically representative of multiracial culture, "because it has sprung *organically* from our history". Singlish's most vital contribution to racial harmony is to enable everyone to communicate with everyone else – and so, bringing everyone together.

Some might argue that even Singlish advantages certain communities – for example, because of the preponderance of Hokkien in its vocabulary – but, this aside, Singlish cuts through the class divide in ways that no other language does.

At its more advanced levels, true mutual understanding can be nurtured if there is first a change in mindset, as Tan Dan Feng recommends. Further adapting a metaphor from playwright Kuo Pao Kun of cultures as "trees", he calls on Singaporeans to go beyond just waiting for natural "cross-pollination" of different cultures. Instead, they should consciously seek to develop "deeper roots and higher branches" – going "deeper" to learn about, and really appreciate, the cultures of other ethnicities, while also going "higher" to find shared, collaborative inspiration and creativity, so as to create "a verdant canopy" (a fertile, ethnically diverse national culture) that benefits the entire "forest" of society.

Second, more face-to-face interaction should be facilitated. Visiting each other would be a big step forward – literally and figuratively – over the "thresholds" of our typically separate lives. "The best way to know someone is to have conversations in the person's home," says Saleemah Ismail, whose non-profit organisation New Life Stories is helping to foster such understanding, with volunteers from all age groups and backgrounds visiting the homes of children of incarcerated parents. Stereotypes fall away, as the volunteers realise that these disadvantaged children – previously perceived as lazy and unmotivated – are just as determined to improve their situation, but it is their economic stress, mental anguish, and financial status that hinder their development, even before starting primary school.

In like spirit, Kua Ee Heok's mental wellness programmes in the community – run by volunteers to help seniors improve their physical and mental health – transcend ethnicity, culture and social class. These initiatives have promoted social connectedness and stirred a sense of empathy, altruism and collective responsibility – "a small step in the long journey of nation-building but a giant leap for communal achievement and pride".

Third, the plurality of racial identity should be embraced. For Alexius Pereira, the Eurasian experience shows this possibility clearly: If Eurasian Singaporeans can come together so well, despite hugely diverse ancestry, then Singaporeans of various ethnic backgrounds can surely do the same. The key is to embrace diversity, and not try to emphasise the superiority of any one subgroup. By and large, he believes, Eurasians feel included enough in society to be able to laugh off being asked by unaware Singaporeans of other races: "So, how long have you been in Singapore?"

As for Kenneth Paul Tan, who is of Chinese-Eurasian heritage, the racially insensitive question he gets is: "Are you Chinese?", which, he suspects, might reveal judgement of some kind. This experience no doubt helps him to empathise better with

The "Geometry of Community"

those who bear even more of the brunt of racial prejudice: "It is one of the most humiliating things to have to explain how latent discrimination limited one's prospects. Many would rather just say they were not good enough."

Like the Eurasians, and those of mixed race, the Peranakans have also been singled out for not being "Chinese enough". As Linda Chee recounts, hawkers belittled her in her youth, as her ragged Hokkien did not pass muster. "The remarks were hurtful," she recalls, especially the jibe "OCBC" (*Orang Cina Bukan Cina*, or "Chinese people who are not Chinese"), a label for the Peranakan community that provided mirth for those who lobbed such insults.

To come to terms with such stereotyping, Billy Steven Tay's personal epiphany applies to all Singaporeans, not just those of mixed heritage: "Being made up of more than one identity was what it meant to be Singaporean." For a long time, he thought he had to choose to be Peranakan or Chinese, until he realised he could be both, and was already both.

The beauty and value of blended cultures, such as that of the Peranakans, or Eurasians, is in a hybridity that is open to change, the capacity always to accommodate and absorb more cultural content. It is this cultural DNA of integration and inclusiveness that equips these cultures to invent and re-invent themselves for the future.

So, it's not either-or, but both. Same same, but different. To marinate this notion further with culinary metaphors cited by social scientists (and mentioned in this book's Prologue), a person from a minority community is not like, say, a piece of "radish" that disintegrates in the "melting pot" of society's "cauldron" of ethnic integration. Neither is it just a piece of *bangkuang* (turnip) in a "salad bowl" that has its flavour blended with the "*rojak* sauce" of national identity.

Instead, each ethnic community should keep preparing its own "prize dishes" — celebrating distinctive heritage and cultural identities — so as to have even more to bring to the "table", to share at the communal "potlucks" laid out within the shared spaces of society. Imagining the forging of cohesiveness out of racial diversity as a "potluck" acknowledges and respects greater agency for all groups, and is much more empowering than a "salad bowl" or "melting pot". Social capital is richest when everyone feels, and owns, such agency.

> **Racial harmony is a matter of dealing with the "Venn diagrams of life", those overlaps between the lives of the various ethnic communities.**

By comparison, a "*rojak* sauce" of national identity would inevitably carry political and other connotations, that a "potluck" of societal cohesiveness would not. The sauce is the flavouring, but it is tasting the final product — the communal consumption of the fruits of ethnic identity — that matters most.

This "potluck" must be based on accepted commonalities around which to build understanding and trust. One such commonality is to "uphold this idea — that being Singaporean is a matter of conviction and choice, and that it takes priority over our other identities and affiliations", as proposed by Finance Minister Lawrence Wong, in a speech at a Conference on New Tribalism and Identity Politics in November 2021, organised by the Institute of Policy Studies and the Rajaratnam School of International Studies.

The "Geometry of Community"

In recent discussions on this subject, the majority community has been clearly told that they have a responsibility to be more mindful about racial harmony. On their part, members of minority communities should also be more understanding. This is something I had already come to terms with many years ago, in empathy with any ethnic minority, when I got over my irritation at being automatically assumed to be Japanese when local tradesmen touting tourist souvenirs would call out *"Konnichiwa!"* ("Hello" in Japanese) everywhere in places like Nepal, in the 1990s, when Japan was the number one place of origin of Asian tourists.

But I was reminded to check myself about this again, more recently in 2018, when I felt instantly slightly annoyed when a Caucasian couple called out: *"Ni hao!"* ("How are you?" in Mandarin) at an inn in the countryside of Cuba, this time reflecting the new primary source of Asian tourists, China. Here was the proud Singaporean in me recoiling at being mistaken as a mainland Chinese, when I would never assume any random Caucasian I see is British or American. I later told myself that my "fellow travellers" in Cuba were just being friendly, and trying to practise a newly learned Chinese greeting. Empathy was called for, again.

Hence, to sustain a harmonious "potluck" requires daily accommodation and adjustment. Editing this book made me realise only now that a poem of mine first published in 1994 carried an insight about this facet of racial harmony from 28 years ago, that has come to be referenced, indirectly, a few times in the essays in this book. The poem, "Close Quarters, Chinatown", was one of a dozen commissioned by the watercolour artist Ong Kim Seng for the book *Twenty-five Years of Watercolour Painting in Singapore*. It

KOH BUCK SONG

was a companion poem to the painting *Courtyard* by artist Khoo Cheang Jin, depicting a scene in Chinatown. Here is the poem in full:

> to modern minds,
> or those of a different
> order of being,
> it must seem
> some kind of science
> to live
> at such proximity,
> to keep one's own circle
> discrete, discreet,
> all the while sustaining
> not too much overlap
> in the Venn diagrams
> of life,
> to understand
> that one is not
> an integer unto oneself
> but a digit
> in a spectrum
> of denominators
>
> these are equations
> some do not calculate:
> the geometry of community,
> the arithmetic of survival

The "Geometry of Community"

The original poem was a reflection on the high-density – and therefore, high-pressure – living environment of the inhabitants of Singapore's Chinatown, especially the bumboat coolies, Samsui women and itinerant hawkers of colonial times. For their significance to the current discussion of racial harmony, the poem's key lines are these: "all the while sustaining / not too much overlap / in the Venn diagrams / of life".

Racial harmony is a matter of dealing with the "Venn diagrams of life", those overlaps between the lives of the various ethnic communities. These are the interfaces between, and among, the spheres of public interaction, and, most importantly, the main esteem arenas of each community. Here are the platforms where people are called upon to contribute to society and earn recognition, while having to jostle against others of different ethnicities. This happens at the workplace where livelihoods are protected, or any place outside the bubbles of home and same-race community – at the wet market, on public transport, or elsewhere in public life.

For racial harmony to prevail, in any society, the key task is to ensure that there is "not too much overlap" in these Venn diagrams. This is because too much overlap is when conflict happens, when latent tensions, past hurts, memories of distrust and dislike, may surface to disturb the present peace. This is the "geometry of community", dealing with the relative positions of shapes and figures in a shared co-existence.

Here, the much-longer experience of sustaining religious harmony might hold some lessons. Religious harmony in Singapore consists mainly of each religion enjoying the freedom to "do its own thing" within each community of faith, while accepting constraints such as refraining from public promotion, and norms such as adapting behaviours when in common spaces, which are kept secular.

A similar model could be the way forward for racial harmony. A key difference is that it is possible to make racial assumptions of other people, at first sight, in ways that would not be possible for religious identity. Hence, to achieve racial harmony, much more restraint and adjustment are needed from individuals. Another key difference is that, for racial harmony, much more can be done, and should be done, to facilitate harmonious relations for everyone, by way of shared experiences in the "potluck" spaces and occasions available in society, which are open to everyone, far beyond the accepted segregated gatherings of religion. This is where there are more options for groups and the state to take action to foster even greater harmony.

Eventually, such accommodations can hopefully become "equations some do not calculate". This is when it becomes second nature to look beyond skin colour, to consciously override any sub-conscious pre-conception. Instead, the instinct would then be to try to see first the good in each person, always treating others with respect and regard as much as possible, so that everyone can then move forward in the ongoing journey towards becoming even more like "one united people".